With Child

With Child

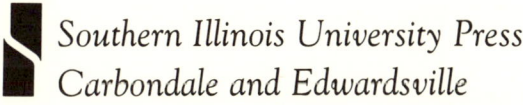 One Couple's Journey
to Their Adopted Children

Susan T. Viguers

Southern Illinois University Press
Carbondale and Edwardsville

Library of Congress Cataloging-in-Publication Data

Viguers, Susan T.
    With child : one couple's journey to their adopted children /
Susan T. Viguers.
        p. cm.
    Reprint. Originally published: San Diego : Harcourt Brace
Jovanovich, 1986.
        ISBN 0-8093-1498-3 (pbk.)
        1. Adoption—United States—Case studies. 2. Intercountry
adoption—United States—Case studies. 3. Adoption—United States—
Psychological aspects—Case studies. I. Title.
    HV875.55.V54 1989
    362.7'34'0973—dc19   88-18423
                                                                    CIP

To Nicholas and Ruth

                        it lies
Within your power of choosing to
Conceive the child who chooses you.
                    —*W. H. Auden*

You are the one
Solid the spaces lean on, envious,
You are the baby in the barn.
                    —*Sylvia Plath*

Contents

With Child

❧ Prologue

My husband, Ken Arnold, and I are in our late thirties; we both have careers, own a house in Philadelphia, and live with our two children. The children have dark hair and dark eyes and are approximately the same age and size— and although one is obviously Oriental and the other looks possibly Hispanic, people frequently ask if they are twins in a way that assumes they are. Invariably, we do not know what to say. "Essentially, but not actually"? "No, they were born in two different countries"? "Not quite; they're a month and two days apart"? We feel almost embarrassed for the questioners. Biological families are so much the norm that it doesn't immediately occur to many people that families can be created in different ways. It doesn't occur to them that the children might be adopted.

This book chronicles our journey to our adopted children, Nicholas and Ruth. It was a difficult journey, but its happy ending makes all that went before not simply a struggle that we survived but a gift of desire and love to our children. The story leading up to our children, moreover, is not unlike what other people experience who face infertility and the inevitable difficulties—both practical and emotional—of adopting.

Infertility was not easy for me. What everyone in the world took for granted as an intrinsic part of being human was beyond me. What did that make me? I was empty; I was defeminized. Infertility grew to symbolize being uncreative in general. And then, what about the obvious alternative—adoption? The practical problems were merely large; the emotional ones—the questions and doubts—were mountainous. What about the adopted children who wanted to find what were so frequently called their real or natural parents? The culture seemed to turn away from the parents who reared them. How did those who were adopted feel? How could people suggest that we didn't really want a child because we wanted to adopt not an older child but a baby, and a healthy one at that? Didn't biological parents want healthy babies? And didn't they have the opportunity to begin with an infant? What did it mean to want a baby or a child? Why not accept being childless? Why did people imply we were racist because we wanted a child of our own heritage? Adoption raised questions of racism, elitism, identity. It forced us to question everything—motives, anxieties, emotions.

We found we changed over the eight years of our struggle to have children. We grew to feel different, for example, about racial and ethnic identity. We changed but never compromised. We knew from the beginning that we were adopting not for altruistic reasons but because we wanted children. Now, looking back, it is hard to identify with some of my earlier feelings. But I frequently become aware of people who remind me of myself several years ago. I belong to a women's group that has been meeting for twelve years; I am the only one in it who has adopted children. Recently in a meeting one woman admitted that she was still uneasy about discussing adoption with me, that she felt she had to choose her words carefully so as not to hurt me, so as not to reveal that for her adoption would be "second best." Adoption was difficult for me to contemplate at the beginning because that was exactly how I felt. Now I know different. I was sterile. My children have given me back my power to create. This book is as much their gift to me as my gift to them.

Understandably, I believe that the bonding that occurs between parent and child is not a matter of biology. A family is forged in love, not by procreation. The trauma that accompanies adoption, both for parents adopting their children and birth parents arranging for their children to be adopted, is partly the result of this culture's emphasis on a literal and naive understanding of the biological basis of family relationships. I believe that our story, as well as those of many other families, suggests that this emphasis needs to be rethought.

The book moves from our battle with infertility to the evolution of our decision to adopt—the steps we took, practical and emotional, our brush with the black market, and our experiences with lawyers, agencies, social workers, and the complications of foreign adoption. The book climaxes in the two chapters that tell the stories of Nicholas and Ruth, the children we set out to find in the first place. Finally, in an epilogue chapter, I explore more generally, from the perspective of the present, my perceptions of the issues raised for us by infertility and adoption. I have kept the names of close friends and family but have altered other names and a few details to protect our children and to guard other people's privacy. Adoption procedures, the availability of babies, and agency requirements fluctuate. This is not a guide to adoption. It is a story of emotional adventure and change.

Although Ken and I lived that story together, our experiences were, inevitably, not always the same. Thus, I have presented part of the narrative sequence from my point of view and part as though written by Ken. Although at times I have used a very free hand in constructing his perspective, the book is indebted to his own writing—drafts of a couple of articles on our experience and stream-of-consciousness responses to questions I posed him. It even includes part of one of his poems. The difference between us—we supported each other, undercut each other, complemented each other—is, in fact, a critical part of our story. Our voices are not always opposed. At times they are almost indistinguishable. That, too, reveals something important about what we encountered.

Wanting children as much as we did is perhaps irrational. There are times in this book when we seem to be obsessed—and in a way we were. But I am convinced, thinking over the years of our lives spent searching for our children, that we were only irrational in the way that people who fall in love are irrational. That giving of oneself is necessary absence of mind. The risks of love and desire are terrible, but we are all human in part because we take those risks. Having children, whether in the labor of the delivery room or by the labor of will, is the glorious risk that this book celebrates.

One

❧ On the Thermometer

Ken We stopped using birth control about six months after we met. There was nothing planned about it. It was the end of 1973. I was in New York working a convention, talking with prospective authors for the Johns Hopkins University Press, where I was an editor. On her way back from Massachusetts, where she'd spent Christmas with her sisters, Susan stopped to spend the weekend with me. I was talking to an author when I saw her across the hotel lobby, wearing her 1940s hat, standing by a large suitcase. She was rosy from the cold outside and looked somewhat disordered, with one end of her scarf almost dragging on the ground and a heavy shoulder bag, bulging with papers and books, pulling one shoulder of her coat askew. Obviously, she was intending to do some work on her Ph.D. dissertation.

Up in my room overlooking Seventh Avenue, we caught up with each other's news and exchanged Christmas gifts. When we made love, it was an unspoken, mutual desire not to use contraception. Later we asked ourselves if we were being irresponsible. But it didn't feel like that. What would happen would happen. It was not that I'd previously pictured myself as a father. I hadn't. I was waiting for the finalization of a divorce from a marriage of eight years, begun when I was nineteen. My first wife had vehemently not wanted children. They had seemed unnecessary to me. We both had careers. Children would interfere with what was implied by the professional, urban life. I had, in fact, postponed an appointment to have a vasectomy only because of a bad cold. The next weekend, my wife had announced she wanted a separation. With that, I canceled the vasectomy.

The summer after the New York convention, I moved to Philadelphia to live with Susan and begin a new job, as an editor at Temple University Press. My writing was also taking off in a new direction. I had had some success writing poetry for ten years but had never managed to publish a book. Now, with Susan's encouragement, I began writing plays. I was ready for new things.

I had always assumed that sex without contraception produces children. There are indeed people whose reproductive organs work in just that way. Movies and novels create the impression that all women are throbbingly fertile, all men bursting with tiny homunculi. To my surprise, Susan did not get immediately pregnant. I wasn't altogether displeased. It made us more relaxed about when we would get married. We were enjoying this time together. I had always before used contraception. This was a new freedom. Making love with Susan quite quickly had become equated with making children rather than avoiding children. And the thought of conceiving a child added a new dimension to my sex life.

We bought a house and were married early the next

spring, 1975. But that event, though legitimizing our decision to become parents, did not immediately alter our childlessness. Susan worried more and more about it. I had never before been so aware of a woman's physical cycles. In the past, menstrual periods to me had simply meant brief interludes of celibacy. Now they were real disappointments. On the other hand, there were a distracting number of other things going on in our lives—my new job, my playwriting, our friends, Susan's teaching, and the fellowship that committed her to finishing her dissertation at Bryn Mawr College within the year.

All the women in Susan's women's group had children. New babies seemed to be popping up every few months. I didn't blame Susan for finding that uncomfortable. The group, in any case, was a good source of information about conceiving and childbearing. We became more focused in our efforts to conceive a baby. A woman is most fertile at ovulation. So we made sure we made love around the middle of Susan's cycle. One of the women in the group recommended highly an infertility doctor she'd gone to named Daniel Meyer. Susan called. It would be December, four months away, before he could see us. I felt sure the appointment wouldn't be necessary. It was a kind of insurance. Like remembering an umbrella in the morning to assure a dry day.

The day of the appointment did arrive, however, with no sign of pregnancy, and off we went to get formal help. Susan had a rather lengthy physical exam, while I sat in the waiting room flipping through issues of *Baby Talk* and *Parents' Magazine*. A strange, pastel, female world of baby powder and Creative Playthings. A prospective father and his very pregnant wife were sitting next to me. I imagined myself and Susan looking like them. Eventually I was called into a conference room, where Susan and the doctor joined me. A model of male and female reproductive systems lay on the table. I liked Meyer. He was friendly, unalarming, and interested, it appeared, in more than ovaries and fallopian tubes. He inquired about Susan's graduate study and my playwriting. He was an avid theater-goer.

Meyer turned to our difficulty getting pregnant. There were steps that could be taken that might be useful, he told us. To begin, he recommended Susan buy a basal thermometer, which allowed for more precise readings than the usual kind. She should start taking her temperature before she got up in the morning. That way she could pinpoint when it became elevated and thus when she ovulated. He would give her graph paper so she could chart her temperatures, when we made love, and when her period started. Our sex life was to become fully documented. The first test, a simple one, would be the postcoital, conducted a few hours after intercourse. It would determine whether there was any problem in the viability or quality of sperm.

The appointment for that test was set up for early morning a couple of weeks later. We made love when we woke up, got dressed, hopped in the car, and sped off to the doctor's office. As it happened, everything looked good. There were, the doctor said, a few dead sperm on the cervix, but not enough to be a problem. We all looked into the microscope and saw the things wiggling on the slide. One or two had indeed passed away. We could make love with the assurance that some of the basics were all right.

The next test, three months later, involved just Susan. The procedure, a biopsy of the membrane lining the uterus, would be done in the doctor's office. Susan assured me it wasn't necessary that I be there. The test, in connection with her temperature charts, could determine if Susan was producing a sufficient amount of progesterone. If she wasn't and she became pregnant, the fertilized ovum would survive only a short time. The results of the test, in fact, did suggest that Susan had a progesterone deficiency.

We were both pleased. Defining the problem so concretely meant that at least there was an explanation for Susan's failure to get pregnant. Moreover, Susan reported after her next doctor's visit, Meyer was optimistic about being able to correct the deficiency. She was supposed to take progesterone in suppository form twice a day for the period of her cycle following ovulation. In the form of a suppository, progesterone was considered safe. There would be no side effects.

Susan April 1976—a perfect month to get pregnant. Spring was my favorite season. Our garden was planted. The daffodils were blooming. My dissertation was finished: I would be receiving my Ph.D. in May. And something definitely wrong had been found with my cycle—something that was probably correctable.

I loved Ken's excitement at the thought of having a baby, but his near vasectomy was a mystery to me. I couldn't imagine how he came so close to having one and wondered if he understood it himself. If I had changed so drastically in what I wanted for myself, I would have examined the issue to death. Perhaps his way was better, but his comfort with change was something that occasionally scared me.

I always assumed I would have children. I loved dolls past the age when it was acceptable and at eleven thought of it as a secret vice. All of my summer jobs through high school and college had been with children. Still, in my first marriage, when I was in my early twenties, my desire to have children of my own was always anchored in the future. My parents' deaths when I was in my midtwenties—my father of a heart attack three days after the discovery of mother's terminal cancer—marked a turning point in my life. In the year between their deaths, my first husband left me. I felt death all around me. I would look at people on a bus or train and wonder how many of us would be alive in a year. Three years later I met Ken. He was a life-force. The loss of my parents crystallized into an intense and immediate desire to have children. No parents and no children: there was a sterility about that.

The irony of Ken's missing his vasectomy appointment was compounded, of course, by the fact that I was not yet pregnant. I didn't want to be overly anxious. Perhaps the tensions of finishing school had interfered. But two and a half years of hoping and trying was a long time. For the last year I'd taken extraordinary care of myself during the second half of each month—enough sleep, an egg a day, milk. I had even managed to choke down brewer's yeast. Each month I had tried hard not to daydream about being pregnant, not to count on my fingers the month the baby would be born, but inevitably I got depressed when my period came.

My work, moreover, wasn't an escape. Even though my so-called field, English Renaissance drama, hardly seemed related to children, I couldn't imagine having a career without having a family. I saw in that my mother's image. My difficulty in getting pregnant spilled over into other parts of my life, most particularly into my writing. Ken didn't understand what I meant when I said I felt uncreative. His worries about his writing related to his fear of not applying himself sufficiently, of not following through. I had great faith in my ability to follow through. What I feared I lacked was the spark that turned hard work into something viable, something alive. I actually dreamed my dissertation had become a baby and was a stillborn.

For a while I had enjoyed the image of Ken holding a baby at my commencement; then, when that was no longer possible, the picture of myself visibly pregnant. Lately it was sufficient to imagine simply that I knew I was pregnant when I walked across the stage to receive my degree. And now, with this new medication, that seemed a definite possibility.

This month, April, I wanted to be particularly accurate about my temperature record, since it was even more important than before that I identify precisely my ovulation. When to start the progesterone depended on it. I'd already discovered from three months of temperature taking that it wasn't always easy to determine my ovulation from my chart, especially when I was in the middle of a cycle and couldn't see the whole month's temperature pattern. If I drank more than a glass of wine, or went to bed late, or slept badly, or got up unusually early, or had a cold, my temperature would be elevated, which would make my chart look like I was ovulating. In the past that confusion was a problem only because it made it difficult to decide about making love. I couldn't imagine going to the trouble of taking my temperature each morning if we weren't going to do everything right. The average man, I'd heard, is most potent when he makes love every two days. That meant Ken and I should make love every other day beginning before I ovulated and continuing until I was sure I'd done so. Now I felt the added weight of knowing that if I misinterpreted my chart and took the progesterone too early, it would prevent ovulation, but if I took it too late, it wouldn't correct my progesterone deficiency.

By the end of the third week of my cycle it was still not clear from the chart that I had ovulated. We'd been on an every-other-day lovemaking schedule for almost two weeks, but Ken had a business trip to New York and had planned to stay over for several days. He suggested that he come home in the middle. We had no assurance that I'd actually get pregnant this month, but it seemed even sillier to miss what might be the critical day. Half a week later, the chart still looked inconclusive. I phoned Meyer, who recommended I begin the progesterone. At last.

Taking the progesterone itself did not prove to be as simple as the doctor had indicated. The progesterone had to be refrigerated, and it had to be taken every twelve hours. That certainly sounded easy enough, but I found it impossible to figure out a regular twelve-hour schedule when I would be home and awake. Even if I didn't let myself sleep on weekends, a seven or eight A.M. to seven or eight P.M. cycle was a problem because I taught classes two evenings at Chestnut Hill College and at least occasional evenings Ken and I were out socially. The solution was to work out a schedule and then, if I couldn't be at home, to carry a progesterone suppository with me. I assumed that it wouldn't hurt the progesterone to go unrefrigerated for a few hours. The only difficulty was remembering to bring the progesterone with me and to take it at the right time. Though I felt I was preoccupied with my body, two times I forgot my progesterone until a couple of hours later. Once I remembered it as I sat in a traffic jam on Philadelphia's Schuylkill Expressway, far from a bathroom where I could take it. I cursed all those cars.

If my temperature rose and stayed elevated, that could mean I was pregnant. As the days went by, I began to be afraid to read the thermometer after I'd taken my temperature. It had dropped very little, and I thought I was experiencing some minor symptoms of pregnancy. I didn't want to mention them to Ken; that would imply I believed they were real.

The last play I was teaching in my Shakespeare course was *The Winter's Tale.* I stood in front of the class of seventeen women and one man earnestly taking notes and introduced the play. Hermione was the most wonderfully created pregnant woman I could think of in literature, Shakespeare's only pregnant heroine. Maybe I'd unconsciously chosen the play for that reason alone. As the discussion developed, I was conscious of my body. I let my arm touch my breasts as I reached for the play on the desk. Their tenderness reassured me.

A few days later my sister Debby and her husband and son came from Massachusetts for my graduation. Debby had little in common with people at the college; it was my parents who would have enjoyed the event. She was taking on herself that role. I loved her for wanting to do so. But the day of commencement was very hot; my black robe, insufferable. I had trouble concentrating on the speeches. It was now five and a half weeks since my last period, but I was feeling less pregnant—the end of the daydream of being pregnant when I got my degree. And I missed my parents. Surely I hadn't gotten the degree simply to please them!

We went to the reception following. I couldn't locate my advisor; perhaps he was coming later. If only one of my friends had also been finishing this year. Very little distracted me from analyzing twinges and sensations. I had begun to stain, but ever so slightly, and my temperature had stayed up. In the last hour was my spotting heavier? The suppository dripped so much that it was difficult to tell unless I actually looked, and I had sworn that I would allow myself to go to the bathroom only once a half hour. I should focus on the party; of all people, I shouldn't be feeling like an outsider.

After graduation and before the summer course I was teaching, Ken and I had planned a celebratory trip to New Orleans. We would take the Southern Crescent down—we'd actually booked a compartment—stay for a few days, and fly back. Now, loaded with a basket of food and wine, we caught the train. Ken liked reading out loud and I liked listening. We chose for this trip *Alice in Wonderland* and, in case we finished that, *Madame Bovary.* We would eat, read, watch the scenery, and talk. My family and I had traveled from Boston to the West Coast by train when I was a small child. I remembered the lulling sound and feel of the train as I fell asleep beside my twin sister, Dorie, in an upper berth. I was looking forward to a night with Ken on the train—and to New Orleans. We had enough money for several "real" restaurant meals and an evening listening to jazz. We planned to do some sight-seeing, take a streetcar (Streetcar Named Desire?) to the Garden District, rent a car, see the bayou country. Ken was well acquainted with New Orleans; I had never been there. It would be a second honeymoon—the dissertation behind and a pregnancy ahead of us.

Nonetheless, the progesterone and my spotting were a constant irritation. If I only knew absolutely I wasn't pregnant and could stop the progesterone, put this cycle behind me, focus on the next one, and simply enjoy our trip. Meyer had said I should continue the progesterone until it was clear that my period was beginning. But what precisely was the difference between staining, spotting, and bleeding? Staining definitely did not indicate the end of a cycle; spotting was an uncertain state; bleeding was an obvious sign. I was both depressed and angry that I was depressed.

A couple of days after we returned home, I decided I was bleeding, not spotting, and stopped the medication. My first try with progesterone had failed.

I had an appointment with Meyer that week. The progesterone could itself produce symptoms of pregnancy, he told me. It could keep my temperature elevated and perhaps postpone the end of a cycle. It was unlikely my cycle had been so long because of a pregnancy, but its length did suggest that the progesterone was working. I asked if refrigeration and twelve-hour spacing were important. Meyer responded that particularly in the summer progesterone would melt somewhat and become hard to handle; that was the primary reason for refrigerating it. As for the timing, I should simply stay as close as possible to the twelve-hour intervals. I would worry less about the refrigeration, but I knew myself well enough to realize that Meyer's phrase "as close as possible" was not as freeing. Here I was, actually able to do something to affect the viability of the pregnancy. The timing of the progesterone was one of the few matters over which I had control. I certainly didn't have control over my body in other ways.

I was bored with talking in my women's group about wanting to be pregnant. Everyone there was sympathetic, but I was the odd one, without a child. I considered dropping out.

At my next appointment in June, Meyer suggested that if I didn't get pregnant the following cycle, I have the next test, a laparoscopy—an operation, but one that wouldn't necessitate my spending the night. He would make two incisions in my abdomen, force gas into the cavity, and look through a lighted tube at my ovaries; he would also make sure my fallopian tubes were clear. I was afraid of needles, let alone an operation, but at this point anything was a relief that would help what seemed an interminable preoccupation with my body, thermometer, charts, progesterone, and making love on schedule. Frances Davies, the woman in my group who had recommended Dr. Meyer, had had the test, had gone on to have major surgery, and now had two children.

The summer of 1976 had arrived. I would try to live like a normal person and think about life outside, rather than inside, me. We were anticipating an almost constant stream of company, Ken was working on a new play, I was revising an article and was scheduled to direct an informal production of a Renaissance play in Virginia. We would be going to the shore in Rhode Island for two weeks and staying in my aunt Doris's cottage with my family. I tended to count my life in summers, more particularly in visits to the cottage in Rhode Island. It was a constant in my life—from early childhood on. I loved the cottage, the sound of the waves, the tide pools. A year was enough time to get pregnant and have a baby. Next year maybe

I'd be bringing a baby to the ocean. My daydreams circled inward. I couldn't escape them.

In Rhode Island, we reasoned that since teenagers often got pregnant in automobiles and on beaches, we should experiment with clandestine, "accidental" sex. One night we went to a drive-in (figuring that was the most potent arena in the universe) to see Woody Allen's *Everything You Always Wanted to Know about Sex but Were Afraid to Ask.* Two evenings later we tried a Burt Lancaster–Deborah Kerr imitation on the beach—hot toddies, a full moon, the rhythmic pounding of the waves. We had fun, but I didn't get pregnant. Maybe it only worked for teenagers.

Back in Philadelphia I had the laparoscopy. The results were not conclusive. The doctor found some cysts obstructing part of one of my fallopian tubes and some evidence of a common disease called endometriosis, which in my case meant that some endometrial tissue lining my uterus had migrated to one ovary. But neither condition was severe enough to be diagnosed as the additional problem that was preventing conception. Dan Meyer recommended that I simply continue for a while with the basal thermometer–progesterone routine.

That fall I began a new teaching job at the Philadelphia College of Art. I finished up a paper for a conference in Cleveland. I met Dan Meyer monthly. In late autumn he mentioned a new step—a surgical procedure, a laparotomy, to clear up the adhesions and endometriosis. The surgery was not absolutely necessary. It might not be productive. It simply would remove the possibility that the irregularities were more of a problem than they appeared to be. The surgery would be major, requiring about a week in the hospital and a month's convalescence.

Meyer did not push me to have it. He suggested I check with other doctors for other opinions or ideas. Ken and I discussed that. Several people we knew recommended doctors, but Dr. Meyer was one of the top specialists in the country and was open about medical disagreements. What would really be gained by going elsewhere? All it would mean was added emotional investment. There was no way that I could make a decision against the surgery—even if it improved my chances only a little.

Dan Meyer had seemed satisfied with the information on Ken given him by the postcoital test, but before I had major surgery, Ken wanted to consult a urologist for more extensive tests on himself. Some men were threatened by the prospect that there might be something wrong with their fertility. I was glad that Ken didn't seem particularly bothered. He was the one who most frequently pro- pounded to people—when the topic of fertility came up—that culturally infertility was assumed to be a female problem, but the difficulties were almost as often with men as with women. It was his turn to do something, and he seemed glad to be doing it. The humor with which he was treating the semen sample, however, suggested that at the very least he felt self-conscious. The sample could be produced in a specially designated men's room at the doctor's office, but he told me the notion of masturbating behind a door twenty feet from people with medical prob- lems—people who might be virtuous as well as sick— was out of the question. In spite of the fact that it was late fall and very cold and the semen had to be delivered to the doctor warm, he would produce at home (with the help of a copy of *My Secret Life,* a volume of high-class nineteenth-century pornography) and then take it over to the doctor's office in West Philadelphia. He wrapped up the sample in a Kraft mayo jar and newspaper, nestled it in his armpit, put on his heaviest coat, and set off to the train. He was turning it into a comic adventure. A day later he talked to the doctor on the phone: although some of the sperm had died, he'd been given a decent fertility rating. The only problem the doctor noticed was that the sperm tended to swim in circles. Ken suggested that was because they had been kept in a round jar. The doctor, he reported, did not laugh, but the idea amused Ken. Perhaps, he suggested, the circular motion revealed something about his personality.

I realized I was relieved the medical problem was not Ken's. Was it that I was glad that another problem had not been added to the list? How would I feel if the infertility were only Ken's difficulty? What if he'd had his vasectomy? I suspected, with some guilt, that I'd be angry with him in a way I didn't feel he was angry with me. If the problem had lain in his reproductive system, I wouldn't have trusted him to be as meticulous about solving it as I was. And I couldn't help feeling that physically producing a child was less important to him than to me. I was the one, after all, who would be pregnant.

When I went to Cleveland to give my paper, I again was near the end of my cycle and on the progesterone. It was a repeat of the trip to New Orleans, but this time without the distraction of Ken, New Orleans, and *Alice in Wonderland.* The morning of my paper, I decided that I was not just spotting, but spotting heavily. I couldn't delude myself into thinking I was pregnant; I stopped the progesterone. My paper was about fiction making: the progesterone was creating for me a monthly fiction that I was carrying a child. I saw everything, even Renaissance plays, as a gloss on my own life.

I ended classes early that Christmas vacation and went into the hospital for surgery. Most of the next week was blurred by anesthesia, pain, drugs. The first couple of days after the operation, I had the sensation of being on the ceiling looking down on myself. Ken began reading *Madame Bovary* aloud; for seven months, since the trip to New Orleans, we'd intended to start it. I kept drifting off; I integrated the novel into my dreams. Ken suggested he stop, that I wanted to sleep, but I liked the sound of his voice, and Flaubert's world of early nineteenth-century France held me even when dozing.

Two days after leaving the hospital, I started to feel genuinely better. I couldn't imagine more positive surgery. It was making it possible for me to be a mother. And I enjoyed convalescing. I could indulge in my secret love of staying in bed all day. Ken waited on me. He put up the Christmas tree in our bedroom. It was a huge, full Douglas fir that made the room smell like a pine forest. Debby and her son were coming for a few days after Christmas. For New Year's, one of my closest friends, Polly McMurtry, and her family were to be with us. I lay in bed, looked at the Christmas decorations, read novels, talked on the phone with friends—basking in their attention—and felt good.

New Year's Eve the two husbands made dinner. Polly and I talked about a night over a decade before when we'd sat in our college "smoker" trying to imagine what our lives would be like when we were in our thirties. At midnight we all toasted 1977. The pleasure of the evening was a good sign for the new year. It *had* to bring Ken and me a baby. Shortly after falling asleep, however, water began dripping through the ceiling onto our bed from a ruptured soil pipe on the third floor. Ken moved the bed and covered the area with rags, and we tried to go back to sleep. The next morning, in the disarray of the room and chaos of dealing with the plumbing, I broke my basal thermometer. I refused to interpret it superstitiously.

The months went by—but with no sign of success. Decisions about when to schedule our lovemaking, when to start my progesterone, when to stop it, how to make sure that my temperature readings were accurate and that the progesterone was taken at the proper time— nothing became easier with practice. The charts had become important for themselves. I would study them daily, comparing the patterns of each cycle. Frances, the friend I considered a specialist on infertility, commiserated: when she was going through the infertility gauntlet, she'd bought her own graph paper so that she could be sure that all of the grids were identical. At the end of each cycle, she'd copied the charts onto new paper, carefully connecting all the dots with ruled lines. Neatness did not count as much as accuracy in the long run, but it was a way of avoiding the implication of the same declining pattern cycle after cycle.

It was getting harder and harder for me to deal with my friends' pregnancies and babies. How was it humanly possible for someone to know so many people who were pregnant? Whenever anyone called and said she had good news, my heart would sink and I would brace myself for another pregnancy. It was such a relief when a friend bought a house or got a job. I began making excuses not to go to parties if children were to be present, crossing a street or walking around a block to avoid pregnant women and small babies. At least one woman in my women's group always seemed to be pregnant. I had worked out what I hoped was a subtle way of fixing on people's faces and not looking at their bodies, but even so, I was careful to position myself so that in a meeting I was not directly opposite anyone pregnant.

A couple of friends in the group kept pushing me to look into one of the infertility support groups. The best known was Resolve, a "Boston-based organization," as it described itself, "which offers counseling, referral and support groups among its services" for infertile couples. I discovered a chapter was being formed in the Philadelphia area. I wrote and received a letter with a map inviting us to the first meeting. It was scheduled for the evening before my freshman research papers had to be returned. I knew I'd be up most of that night. It wasn't good timing. I called one of the organizers and told her I wouldn't be able to make the meeting, but I was still interested. The woman I talked to, it turned out, had also gone to Dr. Meyer but after a year had stopped and managed to adopt a little girl from Korea. She couldn't be happier. She asked me if we'd looked into adoption. She certainly would recommend the Korean route. I told her I wasn't ready to think about adoption, that we were committed to trying to get pregnant and Dr. Meyer felt I had a good chance. He had been encouraging to her too, the woman said, but she had just had enough—she couldn't wait.

I subscribed to the newsletter; it began arriving regularly. It included an announcement column. Beth and John Levin with joy announce the birth of their son, Daniel, June 6; or Jo and Sam Cooper are the proud parents of Jessica, born in Chile, Jan. 1, adopted Aug. 28. It amazed me how many people there were who had problems with infertility. How would I feel in a group of people who all wanted the same thing: what if someone got pregnant? Perhaps being a twin had made me more competitive than most people. The next meeting came at a bad time, too. I let the newsletters and the notices pile up on my desk. I'd get to them.

New acquaintances and strangers, at least those with children, invariably seemed curious about our childlessness. When the man from the gas company, who came to fix our oven, noted the big house and asked if we had any children, I almost lied and said yes. The question came with surprising frequency. I dreaded it.

Practically everyone we knew even slightly was aware we wanted children. We had a carpenter, Will, who off and on for several years had worked on our house. One afternoon he called and said his wife, who was a nurse, knew of a baby boy, a preemie, who was going to be put up for adoption. Were we interested? There was actually a baby in a hospital in the city who might be our baby? What an extraordinary thought. Will said it was all very iffy and that he'd call back with more information. I phoned Ken at his office. He, too, was startled. We had planned to meet for lunch. The baby was all we talked about. He might not be in good health. How premature was he? Neither of us asked the big question: did we want to adopt him? We talked around it. If we took the baby, what would we name him? Over three years before, when we had started trying to get pregnant, we had spent a train trip from Charlottesville (where we'd visited Polly and Ken McMurtry and their new baby) to Baltimore discussing names for children. We had decided on a name for a girl—Ruth, after my mother—but we'd not agreed on a boy's name. Now Ken offered a new suggestion: Thomson, Thom for short. His grandfather's name was Thomas, and my middle name was Thomson. The name intrigued me. Did it sound too clever, or too WASP?

Will didn't call that night. The next day, I phoned him. He said his wife was investigating things, that he didn't really know much about what was going on, and he'd be in touch. He wasn't for a week. It turned out that the baby had died, and he'd been reluctant to tell us.

The school year ended and the summer of 1977 began. Again we went to Rhode Island, without a baby. Ken was busy working on a play about Ezra Pound. I was having trouble writing. I procrastinated by working in the garden. I took pleasure in it. It, at least, was lush and fertile.

It was Ken who first spoke of actively investigating adoption. We were arguing about whether or not I would go to a Temple Press party. Ken admitted that Joan and Walt's new baby would probably be there. We couldn't, he continued, go on living like this forever. It surprised me how easily he mentioned it. I wondered if Thomson had given him the impulse. Could he appreciate how much I wanted to be pregnant? Why did thinking about adoption frighten me? At least if I made some calls I'd be doing something. And if I was going to make them, the summer was the best time. In the fall I'd be so busy with teaching and committee work that I could easily avoid them. Besides, this month for a change my temperature had risen sharply, properly, after about fourteen days. We'd started making love every other day on the tenth day, and I'd begun the progesterone on the seventeenth. A perfect chart so far. Just maybe I was pregnant. Thinking so made it easier to call.

I didn't feel like canvassing friends to find out what they knew about whom to contact. I looked up in the phone book the Department of Public Welfare. I told the voice at the other end of the line that I was interested in asking someone about adoption. I was transferred several times, cut off once, and finally connected to someone who gave me the name of a social worker. When I reached her, I was told that they didn't, of course, have many babies and certainly not white babies. How old a child, how many children (a sibling group?), what kind of disabilities would we be prepared to take on? She'd send us an adoptive parent information form.

It wasn't a complicated application: names, address, race, telephone number, ages, income, kind of residence, and then an open space to answer "What has led you to seek a child from this agency at this time?" I typed an envelope. The form sat on my desk in one of the "To do—important" piles.

The day before school started, I decided I should phone at least a couple more people. I had recently learned the name of a social worker who lived nearby. When I called, she immediately asked what kind of child we wished to adopt. I told her we wanted a healthy infant who would identify with our ethnic background. A white infant? Yes. That was impossible: were we sure we really wanted a child? I would have liked to hang up. Instead, I asked what children were available. The woman said she wasn't at the moment working—she was just out of the hospital with a new baby—but she'd had some contact with the adoption process. At the moment Korea was a difficult source, but some countries in South America were becoming easier. When I did hang up, I was trembling. What kind of question was that to ask: were we sure we wanted a child? Here she was, a new mother—of a Caucasian infant. Why did it mean that I didn't desire a child because I wanted one with our background?

Linda Stanley, a friend in the women's group, had suggested I call the Adoption Center of Delaware Valley; it was the kind of organization that could give general advice. I girded myself for another call. The woman who answered at least sounded sympathetic. Adoption, she told me, *was* in fact very difficult. There were no healthy white infants available from most agencies. There were some who had medical difficulties. What were we willing to deal with? I asked her what kinds of things she was talking about. She told me that even blind and deaf white infants were put into the "normal" category. She gave me a list of agencies and recommended I also look into foreign adoptions. She said, finally, that it would be a good idea to get to know a social worker.

The calls depressed Ken and me both. We were just looking into adoption as a backup, I reassured myself; I'd get pregnant soon.

Ken Although I thought of myself as an independent person, not unduly swayed by current fashion or even family and friends, again and again I found myself precisely in the mainstream. One gauge was the *New York Times Magazine.* Just when we think we are unique, we discover that in fact we are as common as cats. Infertility at the moment was au courant.

I couldn't help being amused that for our first six months together Susan and I had taken great care to avoid pregnancy. Most unwanted pregnancies probably result from the careless it-can't-happen-to-me attitude. More ironic are those cases in which people have assumed that "it will happen to me if I slip just once" and then discover when they want it, it can't. We found ourselves among the more ironic.

Although trying to get pregnant was a mutual effort, the world of the thermometer and the temperature charts was one Susan occupied alone. There seemed to be no way for me to enter it. We mused more than once about the likelihood that men also have cycles that might be charted. Susan argued that once she got off the thermometer, when the whole business was over, I should begin taking my temperature every morning for a few months. The idea intrigued me. Occasionally, I was even consulted on the question of whether the graph suggested she had ovulated or, later in the cycle, whether she'd stopped staining and had begun to spot. I was amazed at the many and maddening variations on the previously simple concept of menstruation. I suspected that I now knew more about the subject than many women.

Yet in spite of my best efforts, I couldn't fully identify with her ups and downs. I didn't quite understand the sensation she described of being tied to an unknown, uncooperative body. I tried to imagine the sensation of feeling ovulation, of knowing an egg was rolling down the tube toward the sperm that I hoped had entered the other end. It didn't work. Susan's reproductive life was inevitably different from mine. I never worried very much about what was flowing through the vas deferens, so long as it came out at the right time and in the right place.

The basal thermometer unquestionably ruled our lovemaking, but I still thought we'd done remarkably well in keeping a sense of humor about it. Nonetheless, it was impossible not to be impatient at times with the regimen. Susan's biological rhythm hardly coincided always with my physical desires. Or, for that matter, with hers.

Some mornings when I had to leave for work before Susan was out of bed, I would lean over to kiss her good-bye and discover that the thermometer was still in her mouth. Since it had to remain there a precise period of time, frequently I kissed the tip. It was my joke. Susan never seemed quite as amused.

One area of my life, at least, was at the moment particularly fertile. My play on Ezra Pound was to be produced in Washington, D.C., in the fall. That meant that every weekend I went to Washington to rewrite and watch over the growth of the play. Because two authors of mine were living there and in the process of finishing their book, I also visited them, usually on Saturday mornings, to work on their project. It was a book about urban living. They lived in the city, only two blocks away from where I had lived during my first marriage. They had three children: newborn twins and a child a year and a half old. We discussed the book while they changed diapers and answered the call of waking babies. It was an odd conjunction of lives. At home, we were fretting about getting pregnant. In Washington, I was giving birth to a play in the midst of infants. I could not but think of how close I had come to a vasectomy. How little we know of ourselves and what we want. I wanted children. I had changed. Seeing how these two people continued their creative lives while changing diapers made me realize how narrow my vision of a few years before had been. I wanted to be like these friends: full of life, surrounded by children, unafraid of taking on everything.

I was glad when Susan had begun looking into adoption. I could, of course, have made the calls myself. But Susan usually got around to such things sooner than I. Also, if I began the calls, she might feel I was pushing her.

I had to admit there was something that attracted me to the often-described experience of being in the delivery room and participating in the birth of a child. At the same time I wondered if that wasn't just a romantic affectation. After all, the child, its being there, was the point and far more important than focusing on one way of having a child. Especially when it was possible that that way wouldn't work. It was, after all, almost four years since we'd stopped using contraception. The last two years we'd not missed one month in our carefully scheduled, and documented, effort to conceive. Would we spend years working on bearing children biologically, fail, and then be unable to work up the energy to adopt? I realized with some surprise that I pitied people who were childless.

I didn't have any particularly well-formulated ideas about adoption—mainly because I seldom had any occasion to think about the subject. As far as I knew, none of my friends growing up were adopted, and I knew of only two couples who had adopted children. One of those lived across the street from my family when I was growing up in Falls Church, Virginia. That couple adopted a baby when I was about ten years old, and I recalled that they, and the child, were spoken of in somewhat hushed tones, as if they were to be pitied or perhaps had done something slightly immoral. I remembered baby-sitting for the little boy but did not recall sharing the adults' tentative attitude toward the couple. It was not a big deal either way, actually, just a vague sense that people found adoption difficult to deal with, slightly foreign. The only other adoptive couple I'd known of was one of my father's old friends and his wife. One of their two adopted children turned out to have serious behavior problems. My father connected those problems directly to his being adopted. He believed when you adopt, "you can't be sure what you are getting into." Thinking of other relatives and of my friends and how they were turning out, I had the sneaking suspicion that you can't be sure what you are getting into when you have children—period. Perhaps that was one of the reasons why in my first marriage I thought I didn't want children.

Susan's first calls hadn't turned up anything, but at least they'd broken the ice. Susan would continue taking her temperature and progesterone, but inquiring into adoption might ease the pressure. We would begin to explore agencies. The other route, people suggested, was private adoption through a lawyer. We didn't have a family lawyer per se, but the lawyer who had handled Susan's divorce and the settlement on our house at least knew who we were. I suggested to Susan that I call him for advice. The lawyer told me he himself couldn't be of any help, but he gave me the name of Michael Bronson, a lawyer with a good reputation who was known to take on adoptions. He was honest, a good place to begin.

From her friend Frances Davies, Susan got the name of another lawyer, Esther Korman, who had dealt with adoptions. This lawyer had actually placed four babies in the last year. Frances had seen her and spoken to her about us. She was apparently quite encouraging. Susan phoned her immediately and gave her our names, address, and phone number. Esther Korman said she'd give us a call if anything came up. It seemed too easy to me, but at least we were on a list.

I was immersed in my play, but it was important that I make the time to help along our adoption investigations. I took it on myself to call Bronson. He was not optimistic on the phone. He said he had not placed a baby in several months. There just weren't that many out there. Nonetheless, he would be glad to talk to us.

Susan and I met in the lobby of the office building in which Bronson was located. We had no idea what to expect. How could we be sure we weren't being taken? What was the dividing line between private adoption and the "black" market? The building was anything but shoddy, but the offices worried me even more. Plush was an understatement. The very walls were carpeted. Long corridors radiated out from the waiting room in all directions. This was going to cost us a bundle.

The receptionist directed us down one of the endless corridors, along which, several moments later, another alcove opened, off of which were several offices. Another secretary indicated we were to sit down and wait. She smiled at us. A smile of understanding and sympathy, mixed perhaps with a dash of pity. She knew we were not part of the normal stream of legal traffic. Were we being patronized?

We did not have long to wait. Bronson appeared at the door to his office, smiled warmly, and invited us in. He began by asking us about ourselves, where we lived, what we did for a living, how long we had been married. As we answered, he made notes. He asked how long we had been trying to conceive and what steps we had taken in the effort to adopt. He inspired confidence, but then I thought of myself as susceptible to lawyers, and I questioned whether Susan was feeling as much at ease.

Bronson turned to the subject of private adoption. Private adoption in Pennsylvania was perfectly legal, he told us, but it was also risky. Once a woman decided to give up her parental rights, there was still a period of time, often more than six months, during which she could change her mind and take back the baby. Not until there was a final court decree could the adopting couple be certain they would be able to retain custody of the child. I asked if he had had any difficulties himself with biological mothers' changing their minds. Bronson said he had not. Before taking on an adoption, he insisted on meeting with the birth mother and, if possible, the birth father. He wanted to be reasonably sure—one could never be certain—that both understood the final nature of the decision to give up their parental rights. If he detected the slightest doubt, he turned down the case. He went on to explain that he learned of "available" babies usually through doctors who knew that he was willing and able to place them. We should remember that he had not had a baby for months and that he had a waiting list of six other couples. He would add us to his list, but we should try other sources as well.

His practice was in probate law. Actually, it was his wife who had gotten him involved in placing children in the first place. He was not in the business of adoption in order to make money, and because his wife handled much of the detail work, they were able to perform the service at a reasonable cost. We should talk to other lawyers, but we should keep in mind that anyone who was trying to make money on adoption should be avoided. His fee for handling everything would be one thousand dollars. Here comes the pitch, I thought. But no. This initial conversation was free, Bronson told us, and we would pay him nothing until he had a baby for us and had completed the procedure.

Bronson was clearly an ethical, even altruistic, lawyer. On top of that he had given us a course in private adoptions. I couldn't help thinking he just might come up with a baby. What if he did and Susan got pregnant? Susan answered that we'd take them both, of course. We wanted two children anyway.

Frances had another suggestion—that we meet Kathryn, a friend of hers who had adopted through the Cradle Society. It apparently was one of the most prestigious agencies in the country and, unlike almost all the others, did have Caucasian babies. They actually matched up parents and children so their background and physical characteristics were similar. That sounded ideal. Susan called Kathryn. We arranged to meet her and her children. They lived in a suburban house and, though not wealthy, obviously had a much higher income than we did. The family itself was no different from other families. What had I expected? Kathryn was effusive about their experience with the Cradle Society. The agency believed in placing two children with a family. So if one were placed with a couple, within a few years a second would be also. She and her husband had picked up their children when the children were three months old, an age when things were legally settled and the agency was confident about the babies' health and development. The only problem was that the agency placed very few babies in the Philadelphia–New York area, and, of course, the number cf people who wanted babies was astronomical. Kathryn and her husband had tried the private adoption route, too, and had actually been offered a baby. The birth mother had been on drugs, and after torturing themselves with the decision, they had decided not to take the chance. Susan told Kathryn about her conversations with social workers. Kathryn's advice was that we not compromise. After all, it would be our child. We should kccp looking for the baby we wanted. She suggested we write Mrs. Hodges, the social worker she knew at the Cradle, explaining that we knew Kathryn, who we were, and why we wanted to adopt.

Susan wanted me to write the letter since, she said, I wrote much more fluidly and gracefully than she did. I wrote a draft, which Susan didn't like at all. She claimed it made us sound flip and self-congratulatory. I struggled to keep my temper. She wrote another draft, which I thought lugubrious and heavy-handed. We worked on it off and on for a week. How to portray ourselves without appearing to be all things? We were, after all, trying to sell ourselves as parents. The final draft we both liked. I typed it up, and we made a special trip to the post office to mail it.

I was glad that was over. I was harried. After a full week at the Press, I would rush off to Washington on Friday afternoons to spend the weekend working on my play. A lot of rewriting was necessary. But even harder was watching other people handle—often I saw it as mis-handle—my creation. Susan came with me a couple of times, but the demands of her teaching schedule inter-fered.

The anxiety of the production was intensified by the threat of a half-million-dollar invasion-of-privacy suit if the play opened. Because of that, the opening had been postponed. The lawyers for the theater believed that they had a good chance of winning the case on appeal. They, in fact, were interested in it as a test case. A suit, more-over, would bring publicity to the play. Attendance would increase. There was something so outrageous about it all that I enjoyed it. Susan did not share my fascination. She was afraid that an agency wouldn't be interested in looking at us as prospective parents if we had a lawsuit hanging over us. We had to appear responsible, solvent, ordinary people. She claimed that she didn't want me to withdraw the play. I should just worry about it more. Hardly constructive advice. It did bother me, of course, to some extent, but nothing would probably happen anyway with the suit. She was overreacting.

The play opened, with a lawyer on call in the audience in case the theater were served with an injunction. It was not. The presence of reviewers from the *Star* and the *Post* became a much greater source of stress. I noticed that the female companion of the reviewer from the *Star* fell asleep. How was the audience to know that I did not want the music, that the first scene had been flubbed? I had no control over my baby. There was a party after the play. Susan and I got to bed at 3:00 A.M. It was a night Susan's thermometer scheduled us to make love. We did, amused at our endurance. It would be ironic if this were the night Susan got pregnant. Perhaps being a father would be easier than being a playwright.

The *Post* gave the play a good review. The *Star* panned it. More rewrites were necessary, so my trips to Washington continued. Susan finally decided her staining had turned into bleeding and stopped the progesterone.

After one trip a few weeks later, Susan greeted me at the door with good news. We'd received a reply from Mrs. Hodges at the Cradle. She had been impressed by our letter and had actually put us right on the waiting list. Kathryn told us that that was unusual. Most often people had to wait six months at the very least. The letter included a preliminary application form. We would fill it out immediately and return it.

Susan started to do so that evening and realized there

was one problem with the application. The Cradle required a couple to have been married three years. We'd been married only two and a half years, though we'd been trying to get pregnant for almost four. In our first letter, we'd mentioned, in fact, that four years. Now what were we supposed to do? We could wait another half year to send in the application, but quite clearly people would see that we'd been trying to have a child before we were married. How would they respond to that? Susan called Kathryn, who seemed, she told me, a little shocked. It was hard to believe we were that unusual a couple. We finally decided our best bet was to write a short letter to the social worker. We would mention the problem, stressing that we had planned to get married at the time we began trying to conceive a child but had simply postponed it for various logistical reasons. All true. We wrote and a few weeks later received a note suggesting that we submit the preliminary information form once we'd had our third wedding anniversary. We studied the letter for any indication of a change in attitude toward us. We were somewhat reassured.

My play closed. The possibility that it would go to New York seemed unlikely. The year withered into a more stolid, ordinary winter. 1978 began. No baby appeared.

Susan   Dan Meyer had mentioned in one appointment that if the medication I was on didn't work, we'd try something new. In March I decided I couldn't bear going on as we had been. I'd taken my temperature for more than eight hundred mornings, had made twenty-one decisions to start the progesterone, twenty-one decisions to stop it. Meyer suggested that I begin taking another drug, Clomid, the fifth through the tenth day of each cycle. Some studies had shown that Clomid and progesterone in concert were successful in correcting my particular problem. No drug was utterly safe, he told me, but he felt that Clomid, under controlled conditions, including a monthly gynecological examination, wasn't dangerous and was quite useful. I didn't need encouragement. I wouldn't have minded if there were risks, as long as the drug wouldn't harm a baby I might have. I was hardly feeling friendly toward my body.

Meyer proposed I participate at the same time in an experiment the hospital was conducting on the effects of Clomid. All I had to do was submit to two free blood tests on about the twelfth and fourteenth days after ovulation. The advantage of such tests was that they could reveal a pregnancy at an unusually early stage. Meyer could monitor my pregnancy almost from the moment of conception.

The Clomid produced one immediate positive effect. My temperature made a much clearer jump when I ovulated, and thus I felt more secure about when to start the progesterone. The Clomid in fact helped regularize me, and it became easier to plan when Ken and I were to begin our every-other-day lovemaking.

It was the blood tests that became nearly the last straw. Though I didn't get over feeling queasy about having blood taken, I managed to steel myself to it. But I could not harden myself to the idea of the tests. Ever since I'd begun with the progesterone two years before, the symptoms of pregnancy that it produced—sore breasts and elevated temperature, in particular—made it impossible for me not to feel optimistic for a while in the middle of my cycle. Then my temperature would dip a little. Each morning as I lay in bed taking my temperature, I'd pray to some power I didn't know I believed in to keep my temperature clearly up. One morning I realized that I *could* take my temperature in the morning but not look at the reading until the evening when I had to shake it down for the next morning. That way the entire day, if the reading were low, wouldn't be spoiled. But whether or not I played that game, my breasts would gradually become less and less tender and slowly I'd become convinced I wasn't pregnant. I hated the sense that I had been deluding myself. The point, after all, was to be pregnant, not simply feel pregnant. And to make matters worse, I had to continue the progesterone—acting as though I were pregnant. I was unnaturally prolonging my cycle and delaying the next one, which just might be the right one. And now the blood tests. People had pregnancy tests when they thought they might be pregnant. Here I was having them when I was sure I wasn't. They were always, of course, negative—further proof that I wasn't pregnant. But, even after the negative test results were in—on the chance that the tests were incorrect—I'd still have to go on with the charade, taking the progesterone, until my spotting finally turned into bleeding.

I was prepared for the tension of infertility to be the worst just before the end of each cycle. But this was getting unbearable. When Ken and I had a highly academic argument over how children develop language and I found myself screaming at him, we both acknowledged with some irritation that the same thing always happened at this time in the cycle. It was hard to express to him exactly how bitter and crazy I felt. It surprised me, I told him, that I didn't experience one of those pathological

psychogenic pregnancies. The closest I got to being pregnant was pretending I was. Didn't Freud record a famous
case of a woman who wanted to be pregnant so much she
created all the symptoms of pregnancy—except, of
course, the baby? There wasn't much Ken could say.

Carol Bohmer, a friend I'd stayed close to after she'd
moved, married, and left the women's group, phoned
later the same night as my argument with Ken and said
she wanted to drop by the next afternoon. When she
arrived, it was obvious she had something to say. She was
pregnant, and she wanted to tell me in person because she
thought it might be difficult for me. "That's wonderful,"
I said, and burst into tears. She had considered not saying
anything about it, Carol told me, but had immediately
decided that would be a mistake. She knew it must be
painful. There was something in the car that she and her
husband, Ned, wanted to give us as a present. She ran out
and brought it in. It was a statue they'd picked up on their
last trip, as consultants and lecturers, to Africa—a wooden
figure carved by a witch doctor for a woman who was
having trouble conceiving. The woman had succeeded,
and when she discovered Ned and Carol were trying to
have a child, she had given it to them. Now Carol, after
getting pregnant, was passing it on.

When Ken came home, I presented him with the
statue. The eyes in the figure were rhomboids. It had a
beard, conical breasts growing out of the shoulders, an
infant slanted across the torso, and another child in the
position of an exposed backbone. Still more babies formed
the legs of the stool on which the figure sat. Angular, long-
waisted, impassive. Ken placed it ceremoniously near the
head of the bed.

Practically every week, I'd be given some kind of advice by someone. One friend sent me a clipping from the *New York Times* describing a study that indicated that women a little overweight were more likely to get pregnant than those underweight. I knew he was intending to be amusing, but it wouldn't hurt, I decided, if I put on a few extra pounds. A letter arrived from an old friend of my mother's with whom I'd corresponded since my mother's death. I had mentioned, when I had last written, that I was trying to get pregnant. Betty wrote that she had talked to several people and gathered the following advice. First, I should stay home and relax. I looked too thin in the picture I had sent her—she was sure I was running myself down. Second, she'd heard of the remarkable powers of vitamin E. I should try that. The third suggestion was that I get a job in a nursery. She also told a story of an old friend who had adopted a baby who had turned out to be practically a giant and who had run off as an adolescent and married a gas station attendant. The adopted daughter had had a baby, however, who was now living with the grandparents, and that child was the "joy of their life." Betty was trying to be helpful, but I wished I could show my mother the letter. I needed her to laugh at it.

Summer 1978 came, and we packed up to go to Rhode Island to spend our usual two weeks at the shore. Aunt Doris, my twin sister, Dorie, and Debby and her family would all be there. In my whole family there was only Debby's child—David. He and Ken had made a pact to eat some new beach food each year. Last summer they'd gathered periwinkles and had talked about eels for this summer. It wasn't only David who made our yearly vacation child oriented. Aunt Doris had been a children's-book publisher, had never married, and loved children. The library in the living room was visited regularly by the

children in the nearby cottages—her "beach children."
Her bedroom walls were papered with their drawings.
Each summer we also got together with Liz Gillman—a
college roommate of mine—and her family, all of whom
I adored and who lived on a farm only about an hour
away. In the old days—between my two marriages—I'd
visited them often; recently I hadn't been able to. But it
pleased me that her two boys still fought over me when
I came. I was looking forward to seeing everybody, but I
needed to prepare myself.

We planned to spend the weekend with Liz and her
husband, Jonathan, before going on to the cottage. They
were having a full house of guests and a big July Fourth
picnic. I decided I wouldn't talk about my infertility; after
all, there were a lot of other things in the world. The
afternoon progressed, and the themes of birth, toilet
training, first days at school, reemerged again and again.
It slipped out: Ken and I had been trying to have a child
for four and a half years. How interesting, one woman
responded; she planned her pregnancies almost to the
hour. What avenues had we explored? asked someone.
Why didn't we look into adopting an older child? Had we
considered the possible psychological causes of infertility?
suggested another woman later in the evening.

Jonathan had rented from the library some Charlie
Chaplin movies, which he showed after dark. I slipped
away and went to bed. I couldn't sleep, listening to the
laughter downstairs—I thought I could even hear Ken's
voice—and thinking of answers to remarks people had
made. How I hated them all. Other major difficulties in
life—health, death, school and job crises, family troubles—
did not occasion such responses. When my father died
at fifty-seven, no one remarked, "That's interesting; my

father's sixty-five, and he's still very active." Of course, lots of people had no trouble getting pregnant. But why so immediately and vocally compare themselves with people who did have trouble? It sounded self-congratulatory. Then the remark about adopting an older child. How presumptuous to give that kind of advice. Would they have been willing to miss the first ten years of their children's lives? But the hardest comment to deal with—and I really had to work on defending myself against it—was that infertility was something in my mind. What did I have to do to prove to people that I wanted to get pregnant? I couldn't imagine anyone in the world wanting it more. It was one way people dismissed me. If the problem could be situated in my mind, then there was no need to be sympathetic: I could get pregnant, if only I could understand the psychological block. I was the one who was warped, an outsider. I hated people.

Ken admitted, when we talked about it later, that he too felt there was something about infertility that made other people pull away, or, as he put it, want to put a picnic table between their fertile selves and the childless beings facing them. That resulted in inappropriate responses. He realized he was offended when a friend of his with four children joked that he wished he had our problem.

We went home to Philadelphia two weeks later—in time for my blood tests. The last couple of months I'd taken the samples up to the lab myself; if the blood was there by nine, the results would come back a day earlier. I left the sample off and, feeling queasy, stepped back into the elevator. Suddenly, everything went black. I was conscious, but the blood was beating in my ears, and I was blind. Someone stepped onto the elevator. What was I to do? How could I know where to get off? How could I find a chair somewhere so I could sit down and keep hidden that something was wrong? The person got off, and there was no sound of anyone getting on. The doors closed. Hours later—it felt like—the elevator stopped, and I sensed a large group of people waiting to get on. This must be the first floor. I stumbled off, and remembering a bench near the elevator, I groped for it and sat down. My head began to clear. Soon the darkness was gone. Even a simple blood test was becoming a small drama.

A few days later I received a call from Carol. She had begun bleeding heavily and might be having a miscarriage. I hung up, stunned and guilty. Had I wanted that on some level? Now what if something actually went wrong? I promised I wouldn't mind that I myself wasn't pregnant, if only Carol's baby would be all right.

Carol came close to, but did not have, a miscarriage. For once, another baby made my own infertile cycle easier to bear.

Two

※ Jonathan

Susan Summer 1978 was almost over. I was not pregnant. Having decided a month ago that it was time to renew our old adoption contacts and to investigate some new ones, we had drawn and divided up a list of twenty people to phone or write—old lawyers, new lawyers, people who knew people, agencies. We had called Esther Korman and Michael Bronson to tell them that the last nine months had not turned up a baby— we were still waiting. Several friends had given us names of people who had succeeded in adopting. We each called a few. One couple had just adopted from the other agency in the country similar to the Cradle Society, the Edna Gladney Home in Texas. They had had a positive experience, but they didn't think it would do any good at this time for them to recommend us to the Home. There just weren't enough babies. Another couple had adopted privately. Their technique had been to write every small-town doctor in Pennsylvania. Their assumption had been that the families of young girls who delivered babies out of wedlock in small towns would not want the babies adopted by people in those towns. After two years, and over a thousand letters and calls (the wife had made it a full-time job), they'd found a baby. Someone suggested calling Booth Maternity Center, where so many of our friends were having midwives deliver their babies. It originally was set up as a home for unwed mothers and thus might have information of some babies to be adopted. That proved fruitless.

I had learned of a lawyer in Kansas who had just placed a baby with a friend of a friend. I called the lawyer. The baby was the first infant they'd placed in six years, the secretary told me, and they had many couples waiting, but she would take our name and address. Ken wrote the Children's Home Society of New Jersey, and we were sent a booklet on the agencies that serviced people in New Jersey. A few of the agencies were available to people in Pennsylvania, but they didn't appear to have Caucasian infants. I called Catholic Social Services to check to be sure they only placed babies with Catholics. I had been right. The Association for Jewish Children had a comparable policy. The list of names and places to be contacted hung a bit dog-eared on the kitchen bulletin board.

The last call assigned me was the social worker at the Cradle Society, Mrs. Hodges. Kathryn had told us that the best time to reach her was on Wednesdays, and this was the last Wednesday before school started. We had sent in our application at our third anniversary in April. It seemed reasonable to call now. We didn't want to appear obnoxious, but we also didn't want to be forgotten. I had heard of one woman successful in adopting from the Cradle who had actually flown out there—uninvited—and made herself known in person. Maybe I should do that. I disliked this kind of call, but I forced myself to make it. Mrs. Hodges was in. Yes, we were still in their files—they would keep our application for one year—but we should know that this year they had placed only ten babies in the New York–Philadelphia area. And they had over two thousand inquiries. We shouldn't count on them for a baby.

I hung up. How could Mrs. Hodges act so distant and say that so blithely? Did she know how devastating it was? The Cradle had been encouraging, and Mrs. Hodges had implied we were in good favor. Failing to adopt was an extension of infertility. My belief in the Cradle was all part of my monthly delusion. I would stop being a health nut the second half of each cycle. Brewer's yeast was cruel and unusual punishment. I dug out a bag of wilted potato chips from the cupboard and finished them up. I looked at the kitchen: the floor was spotted; the plaster on the wet wall was beginning to flake; Ken had supposedly done the dishes last night, but as always he had failed to wipe the kitchen table and stove and had left on the counter several water-filled pans, which by now had been joined by numerous dirty glasses and mugs and a thin, serrated knife of unknown use. The knife had migrated from one kitchen surface to another over the past week. It should probably be added to the bag upstairs for Goodwill. We didn't simply accumulate clutter; we propagated it. Perhaps I was really at the bottom. That meant things would improve. On the other hand, if I was still capable of hope, then how could I think I was at the bottom?

The telephone rang. Maybe it was Ken. The caller was Dan Meyer. He knew of a baby to be adopted, and he had thought of us. Were we interested? "Yes." This wasn't vague and iffy like Thomson. This was real.

A sixteen-year-old girl—Caucasian, middle class, an excellent student at a local high school—was pregnant and due to deliver in less than a month. She and her parents had decided that it would be best to arrange for the child to be adopted immediately after birth. Her parents had gone for help to their family attorney, who in turn had approached his physician, who had spoken to Meyer. The teenaged father of the unborn child knew and agreed.

Where was Ken? When I called his office, I found he had left for his afternoon appointment with an author downtown. It was too early to start drinking, but this was an exception. I poured myself a glass of wine and paced the house until Ken came home, fortunately a little early. I told him my extraordinary news.

As much as possible we would continue our lives as though nothing unusual was going on. Three days later Labor Day weekend began. As planned, we packed up to go camping in northwestern Pennsylvania on some land we had bought. The weather reports were perfect—clear and warm. All the way up we talked about what we were going to do. How were we going to handle our jobs? Ken might be able to take some time off. He had vacation time coming. I suggested that I bring the baby to school at least some days and hire a student to care for him or her in my office while I was teaching. Ken liked the idea, which pleased me. I wondered if he felt jealous that I would have more time with the baby than he, uneasy that I would take on the traditional "central mother" role. I was a little uncomfortable with my desire to have the baby at work. I had always resented people who imposed their children on others. I of all people should be sensitive to that; but I wasn't at all sure I really wanted to be.

Ken was driving. I didn't like driving long distances,

and, conveniently, as a rule I fell asleep after half an hour. Now I felt unusually awake. I mentally organized my time for the next month. I would have to get ahead with my class preparations. I was scheduled to teach two new courses. Now I thought of all the work those courses would demand. But then, how was I to know? Perhaps I had actually brought on the baby by overcommitting myself for the fall: good things, it seemed, came along only when I wasn't expecting them and wasn't prepared to handle them.

We drifted into discussing how we were going to organize the house. Ken proposed making more room in the kitchen for a baby by building a new cabinet to replace an inefficient counter. The baby would sleep in the room in which we'd put all the children's books from my mother's collection. Though we clearly designated it as "the baby's room" when we first moved into the house, I'd never been able to call it by that name. For years we'd spoken of it as the "children's study." That felt safer.

Our discussion came to a halt as we struggled up the hill from the car to the campsite with our overweighted, makeshift camping supplies. How could we ever go camping with a baby? Putting up the tent produced the usual short tempers. We could never remember how to do it. The first time we set it up, it invariably emerged as either two feet square and ten feet high or ten feet square and two feet high.

We saw a buck. I picked wildflowers for our rock table. We ate our meals looking over the distant farms and hills. We took long hikes through the countryside. Back at the campsite, Ken finished reading out loud *Madame Bovary*, begun in the hospital after my laparotomy over a year and a half before. The novel had stayed alive, though at times months would pass before we'd have a chance to read a few pages. Finishing it was the end of a chapter in our lives. Maybe it had more importance than we suspected. The baby we knew about now was the one the laparotomy had promised. We had to finish the book before he or she would come to us.

That baby was becoming very real. I needed to protect myself; getting a baby like this was almost too good to be true. I couldn't let myself depend on it. But how were we to "prepare" for the baby, without "preparing"? The safe course was to make changes that would improve our lives even if the baby did not come. Ken would build his kitchen cabinet. We would have to find someone to help with the house and at least occasionally with the baby, and if possible we'd keep that person to clean a couple of times a month no matter what happened. At least we'd no longer fight about whose turn it was to do the vacuuming. Most important, I would continue taking my temperature and my medication. We would not take a break in trying to get pregnant.

We discussed endlessly what we saw as reassuring signs about the adoption. We had talked to the biological mother's lawyer, Mr. Reed, at length before leaving for the weekend and had arranged a meeting at his office early the next week. He had assured us the birth mother's mind was made up about giving up her parental rights. Both she and her boyfriend were planning to go to college. They were middle-class teenagers who had clear images of themselves and their goals, and they weren't about to compromise them. Surely they were a good bet. The parents of the biological mother were looking into suing their GP for misdiagnosing the pregnancy as a tumor. That mistake had meant that the biological mother had not known she was pregnant until it was too late for a legal abortion. All of that hardly made the biological family sound like people who, underneath, wanted the baby. When Ken had spoken to Mr. Reed about our worry that the birth mother would change her mind, the lawyer had remarked he was concerned that for some reason we would back out. He'd never lost an adoption, he said. He did adoption cases every once in a while because he enjoyed them. He claimed to have an intuitive sense about the people he represented. This one, he said, was golden.

He had told us there were three documents to be signed. The first relinquished custody of the child. The girl would sign it in the hospital a day or so after the baby's birth, when she had fully recovered from anesthesia. The second was the Voluntary Relinquishment form, which the girl would sign several weeks after leaving the hospital. In this paper she would reiterate that she meant what she had stated in the hospital. The last would be the final decree, handed down by the judge between six months and a year after the baby's birth. I blocked out all but the first document. I was sure I'd stop worrying once the biological mother signed that first paper in the hospital. Ken was dubious. I didn't like carrying the burden of optimism for us both.

The day after we returned from camping, the semester began and I threw myself into my courses. I was several weeks ahead in my preparations; I was proving to myself that I'd be able to handle a baby and a career. Ken seemed almost as high keyed, although his style was always more moderate.

We had decided on our trip that we would tell our families and a few friends in Philadelphia, but that we had to be careful about spreading the news—in case anything happened. Everyone seemed excited. With the telephone calls, my anxiety rose.

The more people gave advice about how to handle a new baby, the more I worried that I would never have one. The wife of a friend of Ken's called to congratulate me and overwhelmed me with arguments about the virtues of cloth over paper diapers and rectangular over square cloth diapers. I interrupted several times to say I didn't want to know anything about it, that we had decided not to prepare until we actually had the baby, that the biological mother could still change her mind. A white middle-class girl would never decide to keep an illegitimate baby, she responded, with a conviction that dismissed my anxieties as unfounded—and infuriated me. My women's group was much more sensitive, but still I began to dread talking to people about the baby. I did not want people to dismiss my fears; yet, on the other hand, I did not want them to acknowledge how realistic those fears were. I knew I was putting people in a difficult if not impossible position. Nobody could say the right thing. It was safest simply not to talk about it.

The visit to Mr. Reed at his office was astonishingly matter-of-fact. Our worries about the ethics of the lawyer were assuaged when he assured us that he wanted us to pay only the court costs, no legal fees to him at all. The real expense was to be the medical bill. We were prepared for that. In private adoptions, as this was, the adoptive parents had to pay all medical expenses incurred by the biological mother and the baby. Although I had had Blue Cross/Blue Shield maternity coverage for years, in the case of an adoption, Blue Cross/Blue Shield would not cover a penny of my baby's birth. Not only that, the tax laws did not allow us to deduct medical expenses for income-tax purposes, since when we paid the expenses, the baby would not yet legally be our child. Still, in the great scheme of things, Blue Cross/Blue Shield was rather trivial. And, for the moment, I swallowed my indignation.

Following the lawyer's recommendation, we planned to pay for a private room so that the girl would not be disturbed by other babies and new mothers. Anything we could do to protect the girl. I remembered talking to an adoptive mother (a friend of my sister Debby's) a couple of years before who had spoken of the overwhelming love she felt for the biological mother of her child. At that time, I thought the reaction was strange, to say the least. I could imagine wanting to deny the existence of the birth mother or feeling jealousy or gratitude, but "overwhelming love" seemed excessive. But now I felt something similar for the biological mother of the baby that was to be ours. Was there any way I could show her my gratitude, how much I cared for her? I would be indebted to her for life. I described the emotion to a friend, Peshe Kuriloff, who, in her direct way, suggested it sounded sad, even pathetic. Although I usually took Peshe's comments very much to heart, I was not at all disturbed. It was oddly comforting to identify with that young, mature, sixteen-year-old girl.

We did not intend to buy baby clothes, but Mr. Reed reminded us on our visit to his office that we had to gather clothes and blankets for the baby to leave the hospital in. His wife phoned and gave me the list of what was necessary. The baby was due in a week. We should bring the clothes to the Reeds' house within the next couple of days. I couldn't possibly contemplate shopping for the baby, so I asked Peshe to put together the necessary bundle. On

the way to the Reeds', we picked up from her a tiny
stretch suit, a hand-knitted sweater made for one of her
sons, a blanket, and several tiny diapers. We drove to the
lawyer's house. Mrs. Reed welcomed us and ushered us
into the living room. We sat down anxiously. Mr. Reed
appeared. He seemed pleased about everything. He re-
counted several stories of past adoptions. They'd just seen
the little girl whom they'd helped a friend adopt ten years
before. She'd turned into a lovely child. Didn't I look
remarkably like the pregnant girl in the present adoption? he asked his wife. They agreed that the similarity
was so striking we could almost be sisters. Not feeling
particularly handsome, I wondered at first if that was
some negative categorization. I settled on the more satis-
fying image of sistership with an unknown young woman
who was to give me an inestimable gift. The Reeds would
bring the baby to their house, and we would pick him or
her up there. The thought of holding the baby always
brought me to tears. I forced myself not to imagine it so
concretely.

Mrs. Reed wanted to know if we had the baby's room
ready. I explained that we had decided not to do anything
until the baby had been born and the papers signed. She
seemed alarmed: the baby's first bed *couldn't* be a card-
board box! It upset me that she felt I wasn't acting the way
a mother should.

A week later, just after we'd gone to bed, Mr. Reed
called. "Congratulations," he told me, "your labor is beginning." The biological mother had just been taken to
the hospital. We made love, and Ken joked about our
lovemaking producing a baby the same night. The joke
grated on me, although I didn't quite know why. Perhaps
it suggested enjoying the absence of something I didn't

want to miss—the experience of pregnancy and the birth of our baby. I felt like an expectant father. We dozed off and on. I wouldn't let myself get up and consciously wait for the baby: that suggested too much of a claim on him or her. At 4:00 A.M. the lawyer called again: "Congratulations! You have a son."

He weighed eight pounds and was, we were assured, as perfect as one could possibly wish. But it was a baby we had neither seen nor touched. One day later, Mr. Reed called to tell us that the biological mother had signed, with clear determination, the first set of papers.

We had discussed names endlessly. If the baby were a girl, we still agreed she would be named Ruth, after my mother. If a boy, he would be named Jonathan. We gave our son his name. The hope that we had carried for years had form and identity. He became terrifyingly real. He became ours. In that I felt utterly one with Ken.

Ken's boss took him out for a drink to celebrate his son. I found it so difficult to concentrate on my teaching that finally in the middle of an uncomfortably disorganized discussion about the absence of death and birth in *Pride and Prejudice,* I stopped and told my class that I would be out for the rest of the week because on Wednesday my husband and I would be picking up our new baby.

I became aware that I had been wrong in thinking that at this point I would allow myself to relax in happy anticipation. Ken had been right. A signature was too tenuous. I needed to have Jonathan in our house. Ken by this time was dealing with the lawyer, and I was relieved to be spared that. I needed a buffer between me and the events at the hospital. But I could not completely let go. I nagged Ken to make sure Mr. Reed knew how much we appreciated what he was doing for us. Ken responded that, of course, he had let him know, but added that when he had done so, the lawyer somewhat oddly had replied that it was really his secretary who deserved thanks. She was being swamped by calls from people who somehow had heard about the baby and were offering as much as twenty-five thousand dollars for him. Ken was obviously unnerved by that information. Were we being asked to make an offer?

Tuesday was the fifth day of my cycle—the day to begin Clomid. It was reassuring to take it; it was insurance that we'd get our baby. We began counting the hours: eighteen remained before we were to drive to the lawyer's home to meet Jonathan. Those last hours seemed endless. The day was overcast, threatening. I felt weighted. Ken, too, had no energy. We dragged ourselves to the nearest Thrift Drug to buy a few supplies—only those things that we would wish we had on Wednesday, but not enough to last past Thursday. Which was the better formula—Similac or Infamil? Should we buy disposable bottles? What kind of nipples? It took great effort to make decisions: one box of diapers, a small diaper pail, one six-pack of Similac, two plastic bottles, and two nipples.

We picked up a basket of baby linen and clothes at the Kuriloffs' house. Unloading the car, we were greeted by a neighbor, who, delighted, asked if a baby was coming to our house. That afternoon other friends began to bring by baby equipment and clothes. I felt caught up in their spirit of anticipation, although the presence of those objects, all of them used at one time by living babies, made that anticipation almost unbearable. It seemed increasingly impossible to do nothing to prepare the baby's room. Reluctantly, Ken dug out the portacrib from the third-floor closet, where it had been stored for several years for the use of visiting babies. We began to move furniture into the children's study, transforming it into the nursery I had envisioned, in the privacy of my own mind, for so many years. I knew exactly where each piece of furniture should go.

Mr. Reed called several times during the afternoon. Some problems had developed about the procedure for transferring custody of the baby to the lawyer. Hospital policy stated that the baby had to leave in the arms of the biological mother, and that was obviously something neither Ken nor I, nor the birth mother and her family, wanted. Finally, Mr. Reed arranged, on the basis that the girl was a minor, to have her mother carry the baby, which satisfied the hospital. There were other calls about unexpected but explainable increases in hospital costs.

Frances Davies arrived with several boxes of clothes, accompanied by her four-year-old daughter and her daughter's friend. Both children were bustling with excitement and questions about the new baby and the unusual way he was to arrive. Ken and I stopped moving furniture and sat down in the living room with some wine and beer.

The telephone rang. Ken answered. It was Mr. Reed reporting still another hitch with the transfer. It might take more time than expected. He would let us know if it would be moved from the morning to the afternoon. We settled back in the living room. A few minutes later, the phone rang, and again Ken rose to answer it, though this time I followed him into the kitchen. After he said hello, there was a long pause. "It's all over then?" he asked in a strange, matter-of-fact voice.

We had lost our son: the biological grandmother had persuaded her daughter to keep the baby.

We clung to each other in the kitchen. Ken, burying his face in my shoulder, broke into sobs. Frances came into the kitchen, touched my hand, and motioned to me that she was leaving. I whispered that she should let herself out and drop the front-door key back through the mail slot. Frances slipped out of the house with her boxes and her puzzled children.

Ken's weeping cut into me. "There, there," I comforted him. I, myself, felt nothing.

Ken   A few moments after the call, rage swept over me. What could I do to punish them, make them suffer? I broke away from Susan and called Mr. Reed. With controlled fury, I told him that the biological family must not be allowed to keep any of the money Susan and I had paid for the hospital bills. The lawyer responded that he would return all the money to us immediately. I felt only emptiness. There could be no satisfaction. My impotence overwhelmed me.

It was getting dark. We had not turned on any lights, and the house closed around us. People would start calling us about the new baby. They had to be told there wasn't one. Susan's calmness helped steady me. She suggested we phone our friend Peter Kuriloff, Peshe's husband, who could pass the word on to our friends in Philadelphia. I realized she couldn't go further than make the suggestion. I would have to make the calls. Peter was, fortunately, at home. The conversation was short, and the first step was over. Now for our families. All we wanted to do was communicate information. I called Debby. Then, my parents. My father answered. Suddenly I couldn't tell him, and Susan took the phone and finished.

Now what were we to do? The darkness and the house were burying us. I turned on a light. Susan was so upset by it that I turned it off again. I suggested that we go out to dinner. Susan responded that that was fine, only she didn't want to see anyone or talk to anyone but me. I felt drawn to her. We were wrapped together in a cocoon of pain. I was worried about her. But we simply had to get out of the house, had to do something.

We dressed and went to Frog, one of our favorite restaurants in the city. We parked near the Philadelphia College of Art, where Susan worked. She insisted we walk several blocks out of our way to skirt the school and avoid running into someone she knew. Anything she wanted that would help her. We drank heavily, but that didn't make the meal taste any better. Still, I was glad not to be at home. We were the last diners in the restaurant.

Since there was no way that either of us could go to work the next morning, I suggested that we leave town for a couple of days. Before we left the restaurant, we agreed to go to New York City. Our honeymoon had been spent there.

At home, the night passed slowly. I slept fitfully. At about 4:00 A.M. I was awakened by Susan's sobbing. Her tearlessness had disturbed me, but the predawn weeping was even more unnerving. I did not want us to lose our grip. If only we could sleep. Susan suggested more calmly a few hours later that perhaps some sleeping pills would help. I called Dan Meyer, who prescribed a tranquilizer. Being separated for even the few minutes necessary to go to the pharmacy to pick up the Valium was so upsetting that Susan insisted on going with me in the car. She waited there while I ran in. Back home, while she was drugged and sleeping, I moved all of the baby furniture and clothes into the first-floor bathroom. It was difficult squeezing everything into that tiny room. The pile reached the ceiling. I worked for over an hour, moving back into the "children's study" all of the furniture that had held the place ready for life. I had a vision of a perfectly clean, emotionally empty room. The house became my mind. I would bury the dangerous memories, remove the possibility of feeling, put up signs forbidding entry.

We spent two days in New York. I wanted to be extravagant. It was my way of coping. I reserved box seats for *Otello* at the Metropolitan Opera. When I told Susan I'd done so, she seemed unexpectedly pleased. Although she had been to the opera before, I had not, and there was something appropriately decadent about being introduced to it in a velvet parterre box. We were joined by one elegantly dressed gentleman who seemed to belong there in a way that we did not. I whispered something to Susan at one point, in clear violation of box-seat etiquette, and the gentleman looked at us askance.

The elaborate, ornate boat bringing Otello to Cyprus rolled onto the stage, the rich emotionally textured music of Verdi billowing around it. I was hooked. Susan, on tranquilizers, dozed off several times. I kept my arm tightly entwined with hers, feeling a need to maintain contact, the physical touch a sign of the strange sense of being at one that characterized the whole trip. I nudged her occasionally to keep her awake, anxious that she enjoy the performance as much as I. I deliberately buried myself in the opera.

The next day we saw a play, went to a movie, and had

a lavish dinner at a Brazilian restaurant. I wanted to subject us to sensory overkill. Susan's need for me gave me direction. Our trip seemed a drugged, otherworldly adventure. Our shared exhaustion, a tonic.

While we were in New York, Peter and Peshe removed to their own house the nursery furniture and baby clothes stuffed into the bathroom. When Susan and I returned to Philadelphia, the house seemed empty. But for me, and I knew for Susan, the house was as haunted as we were. Going back to work was painful. It was a jolt not to be in constant contact with each other.

Susan withdrew into a private grief. Some days her body appeared to be uninhabited. She went through the motions of teaching, came and went each day, but had lost the vitality I so liked about her. It seemed significant to me that she was even ignoring the vegetable garden. A deep frost had killed everything, and the brown, skeletal stalks made the backyard look unnaturally ravaged.

I threw myself into my work as a publisher. The fall was always a busy time, during which I had to finish putting together the next year's list of new titles. Inevitably, I fell short, panicked, and then managed somehow to produce (sometimes, Susan claimed, invent) the necessary number. She had always been supportive during my fall crisis. It amused her that I could never quite admit that last year I had gone through exactly the same cycle. "This year," I would say, "I really don't have the books."

Whether I had them or not seemed of slight interest to Susan this fall. When I discovered a manuscript of unknown black sermons from the Garvey movement, in clean shape, ready for publication, my magic trick was ignored at home. I thought I understood. I suspected that she resented my involvement in my work. Perhaps she thought I was being insensitive in not observing a period of active mourning. But I believed in being constructive. I was not going to wallow, nor was I going to allow other people to feel sorry for me. My life went on. The cure for depression, I told Susan, was activity. I also told her to eat more regularly. But that was my normal prescription for everything. Basically, and more than once, I told her that we had each other, no matter what else happened. Wasn't that enough? It hurt me that Susan could not answer.

Usually in the evenings and on weekends, I worked on my plays. When Jonathan was born, I had been revising the first draft of a play called *She Also Dances,* a love story about a girl in a wheelchair and a young man discovering that he wants to dance. I put the script aside after we lost Jonathan and began instead to build the kitchen cabinet Susan and I had discussed. For two months, I worked on it in the kitchen and on the back porch, measuring twice and cutting once, planing, nailing, gluing, and, more often than I cared to admit, repairing mistakes. As a child, I had marveled at my father's carefully ordered tools and his ability to hang doors, cut valances, build shelves and storage closets, whenever the family needed them. Now I was taking on something more difficult than my father had ever attempted. While I did not have a son, I could build a cabinet.

What most disturbed me was how isolated I was from Susan. We fought almost daily about trivial things—the use of the car, the eating habits of our friends' children, the honesty of the typewriter repairman. It was hard to be patient with her. She had lost all sense of humor. Her ability to have friends was something I had always envied. I encouraged her to visit Polly in Virginia or Liz in Connecticut. She admitted that it would help her to see them, but she put off calling them. In the past the frequency of her women's group meetings had sometimes annoyed me. Now I regretted that she had stopped going to them.

One evening, utterly frustrated, I called Peshe and asked her to come over. I could no longer deal with Susan alone. She even seemed suicidal. I left them together in the living room, relieved that the burden was temporarily lifted from my back. And the visit did help, at least for the moment. Shortly afterward, I received a call from Susan's boss, the dean of Liberal Arts, who wanted to know if there was anything she could do. She was concerned, she said, about Susan's listlessness. Although there was no implication that Susan's job might be threatened, I decided that such a threat might just make a difference in Susan's attitude. I discussed the idea with Susan's dean. We agreed that I would suggest, in the mildest way, that the telephone call was more than an expression of concern. When I mentioned the nature of the call to Susan, she reacted visibly. She turned to her work with determined energy. Things began to return to normal.

When the cabinet was finished, Susan was even able to help me put it in place. It was level, plumb. The doors closed. The drawers slid. I wanted to sign it "Ken Arnold *fecit,* December 17, 1978."

Three

Conceiving the Child

Susan   Initially I was sorry I had mentioned anything about Jonathan to my students. In the
months that followed losing him, though, I
became glad they knew about it, for a reason I had never
expected. Over the semester, four students came to me
and told me that they were adopted. It was startling to
discover so many adopted people around me. They
seemed, moreover, to want to give me something. I asked
one student what it was like to be adopted. She responded
that she'd always felt a little older than her classmates; no,
that wasn't quite right—it was just that she knew from
early on that her parents weren't all-powerful. They had
gone through a great deal to get their children. Maybe it
was simply that she had a sense of her identity as separate
from her parents, in a way some of her friends didn't. Was
she interested in finding out more about or making contact with her birth parents? No, it really wasn't important
to her. She thought her brother, also adopted, was also
unconcerned. Another student, biracial, who had been

adopted by white parents, felt differently. She would give anything, she said, to have been a fly on the wall in the hospital where she was born. She knew nothing about her biological parents. I was touched that my students confided in me. They had admitted me to their world, the world of the adopted.

One of the most comforting letters we received after losing Jonathan was again from someone who was adopted—Ned Lebow, Carol Bohmer's husband. He wrote that he could think of few crueler forms of punishment than being deprived of our child as we had been. His parents, he wrote, had gone through a somewhat similar trauma. They were promised a baby by the adoption agency and even got to meet the infant. But the agency was closed because of scandal before they were to take the child home. When the agency reopened, over a year later, they got him—Ned—instead. He wasn't sure, he commented, that the outcome of the story was a reassuring one, but he thought we would be interested in knowing it.

It was my friend Linda Stanley who suggested that maybe if we wrote to the Cradle and told them of our loss and encouraged friends to write, it might help—in spite of our last, discouraging communication. I wrote a draft of a letter. Ken revised it; I revised it; we mailed it. When friends asked if there was anything they could do to help, we mentioned Linda's idea. Only one friend, who was a community activist and organizer, was dubious about the strategy. It was possible the agency would feel we were pestering it, but my last conversation with the social worker made us believe the greater risk was that of being forgotten.

I started looking forward to the mail. It frequently

included a copy of a friend's letter to the Cradle. They were shots in the arm; people cared about us. The mail one afternoon included a copy of a letter Carol had mailed. I began reading it and almost immediately stopped in amazement. There were several typographical errors of a minor nature—but one catastrophic one. "In spite of their problems with infidelity," I read, "Susan and Ken have . . ." I called Carol, who of course wasn't at home. I called Ken. He wasn't in his office. I called Peshe. No answer. Christ! What would the Cradle think! The next time I phoned Carol, she answered. A secretary had typed the letter for her, and Carol hadn't proofread it. She would write the Cradle right away. Possibly, said Ken when I told him, it would seem funny someday.

We did receive from the Cradle a response to our letter about Jonathan. It was from a new social worker saying Mrs. Hodges was no longer working there, that our recent experience was indeed unfortunate, and encouraging us to contact other agencies. A couple of months later, after the Cradle had received our friends' letters, she wrote again, a brief note of two sentences, thanking us for having our friends write the Cradle on our behalf and advising us to pursue adoption as vigorously with other agencies as we were pursuing it with the Cradle. That would be in our best interest. Her "thank-you" did not ring true. Ken and I interpreted her letter as telling us that if we put as much energy into exploring other adoption avenues as we put into plaguing the Cradle, we would surely get a child—not at the Cradle, however. *What* other agencies? The Cradle was an emotional lifeline after losing Jonathan; we had had to believe in it. What other possibilities did we have? The cold discouragement was devastating.

Why were we being turned away? How had we failed to measure up? Had the letters about Jonathan turned the Cradle off? That was hard to believe: the letters were moving; they made clear our commitment to adoption. Was it that we'd been living together before our marriage? Was it that our preliminary application form revealed that though both of us were working full-time, together we were earning only twenty-four thousand dollars a year? The Cradle had low charges, but the agency welcomed, depended on, voluntary gifts afterward. It was a nonprofit organization, and parents who adopted from it were going to feel indebted. The wealthy would obviously be able to give more money. The Cradle had a good reputation; it was a highly ethical organization. Perhaps it was unfair to assume they weren't interested in us because of our income. But why had we been cut off? True, there were hundreds of couples who wanted to adopt and very few babies, but *some* couples got babies. Who were the select few? Had we been in that group for a while? If only the people at the agency had said that they preferred people with more money or who lived in the suburbs, or that after a certain point it was pure luck whom they chose. That would have been hard enough to take, but as it was, added to our loss was a feeling of being judged and rejected. Some mysterious authority was saying I was not sufficiently deserving. Everyone around me had babies. I alone didn't deserve one.

On a whim, I called an old friend who both worked as a social worker and lived in Illinois, near the Cradle. Did she have any advice? My friend said that the Cradle really had many more requests than it could possibly meet and that she couldn't be optimistic. Had I thought of being a foster parent? We should *willingly* put ourselves into a position of falling in love with a child who could at any point be taken from us? I hung up a few minutes later, feeling miserable.

Though it was frightening to think of trying another private adoption, such adoptions at least had one advantage. There was no mysterious judgment involved. Getting a baby was simply a matter of contacts and luck. At least we could remind Korman and Bronson that we were still around. Michael Bronson said he was sorry to hear about our misadventure with Jonathan and that he'd had no contacts in the year since we'd seen him. Both he and Esther Korman said they would keep us in mind.

One day, several months after we'd lost Jonathan, Ken mentioned a conversation with a friend who suggested the biological mother might have changed her mind about keeping Jonathan. That had never consciously occurred to us. We could at least write the lawyer and ask if there were any chance of our taking custody of the child. How could it hurt? Ken was uncomfortable with the idea. He felt there was something pathetic about such a letter. He also admitted that he suspected the birth grandparents and mother had not decided to rear the baby but rather had learned of people willing to pay for the child and had sold him. I couldn't believe that. He let the matter drop and reluctantly agreed to write. There was no reply.

It was during these months that I began feeling particularly susceptible to the suggestions of a couple of friends who were convinced of the value of herbalists and chiropractors. It wasn't that I trusted chiropractors more than doctors, but I was hardly in a position to overlook anything. No one had a corner on the truth market. One acquaintance maintained that what her herbalist would direct me to do would be considered harmless by doctors. In that case, what could I lose? At first I had shelved all such advice. I'd promised myself that if I wasn't pregnant after three years of trying, *then* I'd look into them. Over five years, three on medication—more than fifty cycles— were now up. The friend phoned and said that in case I was interested, the herbalist she trusted the most and who lived in California was in Philadelphia for a couple of weeks. I said I was interested. I knew that Ken wouldn't approve, but if I were insistent, he couldn't stand in my way. I wouldn't do anything that was medically risky. Later, when I found I was not getting around to making an appointment, I realized the basic problem was that I couldn't invest myself emotionally in something I had even less faith in than Clomid and progesterone.

One day while browsing in a bookstore, I came across a book on yoga for women. It claimed yoga could make any woman younger and at peace with herself; it even included a list of ailments that yoga could cure. One was sterility. "The practice of yoga," I read, "has so often had some beneficial effects on sterile couples that women sometimes say facetiously that they fear to take it up lest they become pregnant." Even if I didn't believe that, I had to buy the book. For a couple of months I worked on the Eagle pose, the Shoulderstand, the Bow, the Fish, the Aswini-mudra, the Spinal Twist—all listed as correctives for infertility. The exercises at least helped my back—not a total loss.

We added one other folk theory to our efforts to get pregnant—the lunar theory, according to which the most likely time for conception in a cycle could be determined by a complicated monthly calculation of the moon. Frances was the proponent of that theory. She was convinced her daughter's conception occurred on the lunar schedule. What was attractive about such a theory was that it offered one more possibility each month for conception. The disadvantage was that it meant still another chart to keep up to date. Ken tried a folk remedy himself. On the possibility that Jockey shorts constrict the testicles and inhibit the growth of healthy sperm—a theory we'd heard somewhere—he stopped wearing underwear during the critical periods of the month.

Nothing did any good. The thermometer, Clomid, progesterone, optimism-then-bitter-pessimism cycles continued with little differentiation. I wasn't even getting used to the blood tests. My veins were collapsing, and it was becoming difficult for the nurse to find a suitable source of blood. I felt I was battling a terminal disease.

One day in March—1979—six months after Jonathan, things were especially bleak. It was cold and rainy and Monday. Sebastian, one of our cats, was sick—my favorite, who slept, purring lightly, on my desk while I worked and always greeted my arrival home perched on the newel post by the front door. I recognized the signs: he wasn't in immediate danger, but I'd have to take him to the vet again within the next day or so. The house seemed unusually grubby. Two doors now had fallen off their hinges— and it would take us months, I knew, to get them fixed. I'd been up very late correcting freshmen compositions but hadn't finished the group I'd promised to return. I had a 9:00 A.M. appointment for the first of my two blood tests, after which I had to rush off to student conferences and classes. Ken seemed impatient and ill-humored. Why in the world did I get upset about unhinged doors on a Monday morning, he complained. It would help, I returned, if one door weren't to the bathroom—and it was damned cold taking a shower in a bathroom without a door. We grabbed breakfast, got our things together, and climbed into the car. About a mile from the house, the car broke down. We abandoned it at a nearby gas station and trudged home in silence. It was the last straw. There was no way I could get to my appointment in time for the blood test to be processed on schedule. I had missed the commuter train that would get me to school on time. I knew I was not pregnant. Why continue the charade? It was grotesque, a gratuitous torture. I called Dan Meyer and said for the first time I simply could not make it. Ken caught the trolley to the office, and I took the train to work, late.

At my appointment two days later I was spotting, and I admitted to Dan Meyer that I was unbelievably depressed by the whole business. Meyer was sympathetic; he suggested skipping the blood tests, dumping all medication, even retiring the basal thermometer for a month or two. I said I felt I had failed: Meyer rejoined that if anyone had failed it was he—but it wasn't all over yet. Ken and I simply needed a vacation from all of it: drugs, tests, charts, discipline, anxiety.

A couple of weeks later, the dean interrupted one of my freshman English classes with a student whom ten minutes before I had ordered out of the room for interrupting the class repeatedly and being rude. I stepped into the hall and explained how off-the-wall the student had acted in class. While I was talking, I suddenly felt a profuse flow of blood. My survive-and-avoid-embarrassment mechanism took over. The dean agreed with me, apologized for the interruption, and I returned to class. For the next two and a half hours (a second group of students arrived before I could escape), I remained seated in a chair in front of the room and managed to keep discussing their papers. I stayed seated until all of the students had gone, enduring even the inevitable stragglers who remained to ask questions or, worse yet, to chat. When the room was finally empty, I got up, put on my coat, wiped up the blood with a stack of blue books I found on the windowsill, threw the whole mess into a ladies'-room trash bin, and drove home. It was an adolescent nightmare come true; I was once again at puberty, frightened by my body, but even more by the thought of exposure.

The bleeding stopped as quickly as it started, but after a few days it began again and continued, at times lighter than others, for several weeks. Since I had decided to take a vacation from worrying about my body, I did not immediately call the doctor. After all, my system was probably just reacting to the shock of being off medication. When the situation did not improve, Ken urged me to check with Dan Meyer, who, after examining me, recommended a D and C. Meyer explained it as a minor surgical procedure in which the cervix is dilated and the uterus scraped. Another operation, another recovery room.

Shortly after I awoke from the anesthesia, Dr. Meyer came into the recovery room and told me that there was evidence I had been pregnant. I had had a miscarriage. He obviously took it as a good sign, and I did too. It was the first clear evidence that I could become pregnant. I simply couldn't let myself feel guilty about stopping the medication when I did: the bleeding during the progesterone cycle probably indicated that the pregnancy would not have worked anyway. But if I could get pregnant once, it could happen again.

Ken Three years before, Susan and I had gone out to dinner to celebrate my birthday. We had had a good meal. We were going to kill our month's budget and order liqueurs, but first Susan excused herself to go to the ladies' room. While she was gone, I decided to have a cigar. After all, it was my birthday. It was only decent to ask the couple at the next table if it would bother them. I sensed something about the man that made me think it wouldn't. I was right. He pulled out four expensive cigars, named and described them, offered me one, and asked me if I'd be interested in joining a gourmet group they were starting. They'd been watching us eat, he said. He then introduced his wife, Marlene, and himself, Joe-Blume. The hyphen, he explained, added "a little dash" to his name. When Susan returned, I introduced her and told her of the invitation. She was not as amused as I. We were busy enough as it was, she said later. I enjoyed the idea. Besides, it would be unlikely that Joe would actually call us. Later, after I knew Joe-Blume, I would have been surprised if he hadn't.

A few weeks after the dinner, we went to an organizing meeting. The other people, all old friends of Joe and Marlene's, claimed they were a bit dubious about this new couple Joe had picked up in a restaurant. But we were clearly accepted. And so the gourmet group started. It turned out to be the only group with which we associated that was totally childless. All were professional, Center City people who had chosen not to have children. It was a break for me, and I knew for Susan, too. We made all kinds of meals—French, Mexican, German, Japanese, Italian, Armenian. The only requirement seemed to be that each dish take at least four hours to make. Susan and I once spent a whole afternoon making eggs-in-aspic. I wasted five eggs perfecting my technique of poaching eggs free form. Then we poured layer after layer of seasoned gelatin over the eggs to make a deep glaze. Finally, Susan decorated the dish with pimento roses and tiny branches made of leek greens. No one much liked how it tasted, but it was visually a masterpiece.

Joe was a remarkable source of information about everything in Philadelphia. I suggested he would be a good person to call about adoption contacts. When I phoned, Joe immediately said he would talk to a couple of lawyers he knew and get back to me. The next day, he called to say he'd talked to a lawyer friend who contacted a second lawyer who had, right then, a client about to give birth. It was apparently a slightly touchy situation. If there were any chance that this baby might be adoptable, the second lawyer would call me. Joe did not know that lawyer's name, only that we would be hearing from him if he thought something could be worked out.

I certainly trusted Joe, but the whole thing sounded suspiciously secretive. About a week later, I got a call from a lawyer who did not give his name but identified himself as a friend of Joe-Blume's friend. He described the situation. His client was a drug addict currently in jail awaiting trial. She was pregnant. Since this was his client's second offense—she was up on a robbery charge—he thought she would probably be sentenced to a fairly lengthy term. She wanted to place the baby for adoption. Were we interested? I asked for more information. Did she have other children? Yes, she had previously borne a child, whom she had kept. That did not sound good. What about the financial arrangements? The state would pay the hospital costs, since the mother was in custody. The lawyer told me, however, that his client was wondering whether adopting parents would consider paying the legal fees for her defense, since they wouldn't be responsible for the medical bills. I said we would have to think about it. The lawyer replied that he needed to know quickly and would call me back in a day for our answer.

Susan and I talked about it. We were uneasy about the mother's health. And was the plan to place the child for adoption all a ruse? Was the birth mother intending to take the baby back after she got out of jail? After all, she had kept the other child. I called Michael Bronson and described the situation to him. Bronson told me that our paying for the mother's legal fees in exchange for the baby was an illegal arrangement. We shouldn't touch it on those grounds alone. We definitely did not want to get into the black market. When the lawyer called back, I told him we were not interested.

At this point, Peshe and Peter mentioned a friend whose cousin was a lawyer who also handled adoption cases. Susan phoned the friend. He recommended his cousin highly. I called him.

Sidney Popper was an expansive, enthusiastic person on the phone. He instantly said that we should come right in to see him. I made an appointment for the next day. Popper's office was slightly less posh than Bronson's. His walls were covered with paintings of ducks. He wore a loud bow tie. (I had never trusted men who wore bow ties.) We settled down across the desk from him. Our experience with Bronson made me confident that I knew how these things worked. Once again we were there for an hour. The difference was that Popper did most of the talking. He told one story after another about his successes in placing babies. They were good stories. They all had happy endings. I mentioned where I worked. It turned out we had an acquaintance in common. One of my series editors, Charles Davidson, had gone to college with Popper. He exclaimed that the three of us would have to get together one day for lunch. Before we left, we learned that Popper had a contact in Colombia, a lawyer who had successfully managed to come up with babies for him. He added that the last baby from Colombia was fair and only six months old. He asked if we would be interested. "Yes, certainly." I left feeling encouraged, in spite of the bow tie. Susan said she was too, although she did not like Popper at all.

The next week, Popper called Charles and suggested we all three meet downtown the next week. Charles was amused by the idea, although he was not part of the old-boy college network that Popper obviously relished so much. Popper arranged to meet us at one of the exclusive men's clubs in Philadelphia. As we sat down, he mentioned to me that he had written to his lawyer contact in Colombia and expected to have some information for us soon, although Colombians tended to be slow in responding. "Soon" could mean three or four months. Most of the lunch was spent talking about Charles and Popper's old college chums. I rather liked being an outsider.

A few weeks later, my old next-door neighbors in Baltimore, Tommye and John Allen, called. I had always considered them among the most colorful people I knew. I enjoyed their penchant for the flamboyant and the dramatic, and their sense of humor. On one occasion, Susan and I had visited them in their shore place on the Severn River and had found ourselves assisting in a wedding at which John was officiating. He had been ordained a few years before in order to marry two friends and, subsequently, had performed weddings for the fun of it. The couple in this case had come to him after the local Lutheran minister had suggested they live together until he could return from a vacation to perform the ceremony. The people were shocked and had turned to John for help. I filmed the proceedings with a Kodak movie camera. Susan ran the record player, on which suitable wedding music played. My final assignment was to write the names of the bride and groom on their car with whipped cream.

Susan had mentioned our efforts to adopt in a Christmas note. Tommye told me she knew some people back in Mississippi, where she was born and raised, who had some contacts in the adoption business. If we would like her to, she promised to check into them. A few days later she called with a couple of names. One was a woman connected with something called the Adoption Unit in Jackson, Mississippi. Tommye suggested we write to her. She also gave us the name of a lawyer who she learned had placed babies in the past.

Later that evening, on an impulse, I picked up the phone and called the lawyer. I identified myself and said that we were looking to adopt and understood that he occasionally served as an intermediary in adoptions. We wanted a baby? the lawyer replied. How soon?

He went on to give the details. A young woman in Texas was pregnant. She had engaged him to place her baby. The arrangement was that we would have to pay for her room and board for two or three months, plus her hospital costs. With legal fees and transportation costs (the lawyer planned to move her to Mississippi), the total fee came to something in the neighborhood of twelve thousand dollars. I listened, asked a few questions, and said I would call back. The lawyer urged that we make a decision quickly.

It sounded fishy and was certainly expensive. There were lots of unanswered questions. For example, why did we have to put her up for three months? Why couldn't she stay in Texas? It might be that private adoptions were illegal in Texas. But did that mean that it was legal to move her out long enough to give birth? The lawyer's fee was around five thousand dollars, clearly too large.

Nonetheless, we decided to look into it a bit further. Bronson was out of town, so I called Popper and asked if he could check on this Mississippi lawyer's credentials and write him on our behalf. I figured that if anything were drastically wrong, or if the arrangement were illegal, our bringing our own lawyer into the picture would scare away the Mississippi lawyer. Popper checked the Martindale-Hubbell Law Directory ratings for the lawyer in Jackson and wrote to tell us that he had a good rating for ethics, although not such a good one as a practitioner. He wrote to the lawyer on our behalf, asking for further details and that it be noted that he, Popper, was officially representing us.

In the meantime, we talked about whether we were crazy to consider this option at all. It would be very hard for us to handle the cost. At the same time, Bronson and Korman didn't seem to be coming up with a baby, and the Cradle was closed to us. I was inclined to think we should just go ahead, get it over with. One evening, Susan was out and I was watching two television shows at the same time. Both were so dull I could change the channels back and forth without missing anything. I kept thinking of the baby in Texas. On the spur of the moment I decided to call my father to ask his advice, something I almost never did. I called and described the problem. My father said that it sounded odd to him and certainly expensive. To be more accurate, it actually sounded crooked. He would stay out of it. It was rare for me to get a clear, unequivocal recommendation from my parents. I realized that he was right. When Susan got home, I talked to her and she, too, agreed. The next day, I phoned Popper to tell him to withdraw on our behalf.

Peter had another suggestion. He had discovered that an associate, Michelle Blake, had adopted from the Edna Gladney Home, the agency considered so similar to the Cradle Society. Michelle had told Peter she'd be glad to talk to us. Susan called her. Michelle invited us to a dinner party to which the Kuriloffs were also coming. When we arrived at the Blakes' comfortable suburban home, again we were aware that theirs was quite a different income bracket. Michelle's husband was a businessman, a salesman for a company, he explained in detail to me, that manufactured checks and deposit slips. Michelle was sympathetic to our story of our efforts to adopt. She suggested we write and tell the Gladney Home that we were friends of hers. She would also write the agency on our behalf. Susan revised the letter we had written initially to the Cradle and sent it off. A few weeks later we received a note saying our letter was appreciated, but the Gladney Home was not at the moment taking on any new adoptive parents.

Susan

Summer 1979 arrived. Again, I had time to work on adoption contacts. We had several things to celebrate. I had been offered a tenure-track assistant professorship and had a long article published, and Ken had been awarded an O'Neill Fellowship for his current play, *She Also Dances.* For five weeks he'd be up in Connecticut, exposed to other writers, directors, critics, set designers, and actors. His play would be produced, as a script-in-hand reading, by major-league professionals. It was a break into the "real" theater world. We'd have to call a vacation from trying to get pregnant for at least one cycle. But I would be able to visit him; he'd be less than an hour from our cottage in Rhode Island.

The summer, however, loomed ahead like a black hole. Ken was wrapped up in his play. I usually felt I was an important influence on his writing, but not at the moment. And my own writing wasn't going at all well. Somehow, I hadn't been able to shake off the stillbirth of my dissertation. Then one day after Ken left for Connecticut, my cat Sebastian, my child surrogate, suddenly died.

I felt I should take advantage of a freer schedule and visit Polly and Ken McMurtry, who had just moved to Vermont. When their second child was born in the winter, Polly hadn't called us for over a month. I knew it was hard to tell a friend good news when you thought it might be at least partially painful. It was important I see Polly; I was building walls around myself. I had a dream in which I was a Navaho sentenced to build a city of adobe walls. I was alone building them. I started constructing them underground. I never saw anybody, I didn't know why I was doing it, and I couldn't figure out whether I was on the outside or the inside of the walls.

More months and cycles had passed—thermometer, Clomid, progesterone, charts, blood tests. No baby was closer. The only possible relief was to try to focus on new adoption contacts. I wrote to the Adoption Unit in Jackson, Mississippi, and promptly received a note saying the agency didn't deal with people outside Mississippi. A friend had mentioned an organization named the County Medical Society. I wasn't sure what that was, but I wanted to try everything. I left a message, and the call was returned. No, they couldn't be of any help. Debby, in Massachusetts, checked into adoption there. Catholic Services there placed babies with non-Catholics; there was about a three-year wait for prospective parents. They, however, could not work with someone in Pennsylvania. I called Catholic Social Services in Philadelphia. No, their policy was what I had been told previously; they just placed babies with Catholics, and churchgoing Catholics at that. On Debby's suggestion, I wrote to Miss Bloom, a hospital administrator who had worked under my father to see if she had any contacts or advice. I couldn't help thinking— maybe incorrectly—that if my father were alive, with all his connections in the medical field, somehow a baby would have been found for us. But my father had been dead ten years, and I had lost touch with almost all his professional associates. Miss Bloom wrote back a note that I interpreted as indicating she wasn't going to be of any help. While my father was alive, Miss Bloom would have done anything to help out the Viguers family. I'd grown up with parents who had contacts; I was simply joining most of the world now. Why should I be privileged? But I kept meeting or hearing of people who were. I'd talked to a woman recently at a party who had adopted two babies privately—and quickly. I asked her if anyone in her family was a doctor. Yes, she said, both her father and her husband.

What about foreign adoptions? We were interested in Popper's suggestion of Colombia, but still, why were we so slow in extending our options? Catholic Social Services would not place American babies with non-Catholics, but I found they would place foreign children with them. There were of course obvious practical reasons behind that, but from another angle the implications were strange: they wanted the souls of American babies to be saved, but it didn't matter about foreign babies?

I remembered a young woman who'd said to me at a party in a context I couldn't remember that she planned to have two children of her own and then adopt one from a foreign country. There were so many unwanted babies, and she wanted to help one. It was clear as she talked that for that woman adoption was an act of charity. That child was not conceived as "one of her own." I said I was not at all aware of vast numbers of unwanted available babies. Adoption also didn't seem to me to be doing good. At least, I wasn't thinking of it that way myself. We were looking into adoption because we wanted our own children. And wanting children was hardly an altruistic impulse; it seemed quite selfish, at least in some ways. How many people bore children to benefit the world? The most successful parents of even hard-to-adopt children were the ones, I believed, who were adopting those children from a need in themselves.

Ken kept saying we wanted children who looked like us, but the truth was I didn't really care about that. I'd always desired straight, dark hair, and that didn't fit either of our genes. It would be rather nice to have a child who had some of the physical qualities I'd wanted. But the idea of a child who obviously was ethnically different was another matter. How would it feel to hear people register surprise when my child called me mother? I imagined I would get used to it, but what if my child felt different? How important was one's ethnic background? If only our child could identify ethnically in *some* way with us.

One line of Ken's ancestors went west and, he claimed, intermarried with Native Americans. That gave him a little—remote—Native American blood, and at times I imagined I could see it in the particular cast of his eyes. Even that was enough to make adopting a Native American attractive. There would be at least a symbolic connection. Ken liked the idea too. I had a college friend in medical school in Denver, an area where there were many Native Americans. I phoned her; Diana said she would look into things right away and call back. She did. The Native American route, she felt, was not productive to pursue. The babies were not being placed outside their tribes.

I had written off some weeks before to Foreign Adoption Resources, for their booklet listing agencies and contacts for foreign adoption, supplemented by periodic updates. There were, I discovered when it arrived, hundreds of contacts through which foreign adoptions could be pursued. But it was impossible to tell how risky those contacts were, how convoluted the legal processes. Some countries, I knew, were more receptive than others to their babies' being adopted by foreigners, but nothing was stable; countries easily changed their policies.

What worried me most was the question of the child's health. What risks of that sort were involved in a foreign adoption? The previous summer I had met a woman who had adopted, three years before, a two-year-old Chilean child. The child had been in terrible condition: in fact her trip to the States had been postponed because she had meningitis. She was now fine, but when they'd received her, she hadn't walked or talked; her development had been that of a baby, rather than a two-year-old. Actually, the mother said, that gave them the opportunity to experience all the stages of her development. They felt they'd missed virtually nothing; they were very lucky. I had shivered. It was hard to imagine being glad your child was so behind at the beginning. What if she hadn't caught up? Wouldn't you always worry something was wrong? I wanted a baby who was developmentally normal. Was it so strange to want that? What mother bearing a child biologically wanted a child with a developmental problem? But it all made me uncomfortable with myself.

There was one major advantage to foreign adoptions: there would be no possibility of birth parents tracking down children. I'd begun to hear horror stories about that. A friend of a friend adopted a child, and three years later the birth father presented himself in the same small town in Maine and began pestering the child. There also couldn't be the crisis we experienced with Jonathan.

It was time to see what babies were available. The place to begin was probably the major agencies dealing with foreign adoptions; with those agencies there would be a minimum of risk. The three that had been mentioned to me again and again were Holt in Oregon, Dillon in Oklahoma, and Welcome House, much closer to home, in Doylestown, Pennsylvania. I knew people or had names of people who had adopted from all three. Different people said different things about them. Some said one was more flexible than another, or quicker, but even those impressions varied depending on whom I talked to. I wrote them all, and their literature soon arrived. Dillon just had Korean children, required that the adoptive couple be married four years—which was no longer a problem for us—and was clearly a church-related organization. I wasn't sure why that last bothered me so much. I wasn't religious, but that need not prevent me from investigating Dillon. I would feel fraudulent, though. And how would we handle the agency's interest in "the adoptive family's involvement in their local church"? Holt was even more explicitly Christian oriented. It clearly preferred people who knew "God's love through Jesus" and requested a "statement of faith" from its applicants. It also required, except in "unusual circumstances," that the wife take a six-month leave of absence from work. No one told a mother giving birth that she couldn't have her baby unless she took a six-month break from her job. Of course it might be necessary—with either a birth or adopted child—but it was upsetting to think of working with an agency that would tell you what to do, that would oversee your parenting.

I knew the most about Welcome House, which like Dillon dealt only with Korean children. I'd met two children adopted through them. But that agency stated that at this time they would accept only couples who would consider a child up to the age of two years. That was ancient. Ken and I wanted a baby! Their reason, moreover, for saying two years—that it frequently took until that age for the processing in Korea to be completed—made me wonder if a comparable age wasn't also characteristic of the children adopted through the other two agencies. There was one other paragraph in the Welcome House literature that disturbed me. "We are unable," the cover letter read, "to accept applications from families who limit their choice to a child who is half American Caucasian. . . . Since our focus is on the needs of the children, and since we believe that the child of half Korean heritage thrives best in a home that would have welcomed him had he been fully Korean, we are able only to accept homes for children where a child of a full Oriental as well as Oriental-Caucasian background would be welcome." Here again was an agency suggesting that if you wanted your child to share at least partially your racial heritage, you would be ashamed of or at least uncomfortable with the Korean part of the child. I didn't feel that way: the Korean part of a Korean-Caucasian child would be a special part, one to be cultivated as separate from ourselves—I rejected, after all, the idea of children being extensions of their parents. But the Caucasian part would mean the child's racial identification would not be entirely with another culture. He or she would have a foothold in our racial world. The letter made me defensive. I wasn't measuring up.

The Dillon, Holt, and Welcome House application forms sat on my desk. Before I drove to Rhode Island, I filed them away. I knew where they were if we needed them.

Rhode Island was lonely. Ken came for only a couple of overnight stays. The next-door family of parents and five children, now grown, with whom as a child I had played in the summers, could always be depended on to have at least one new baby. This summer they had three. I worked on a new course, which I was scheduled to teach in the fall, and attempted a new article. I visited Liz and her family at their new farm. I met Polly's new baby, a cherubic six-month-old. I left the car with Ken and took the train home. The next weekend, Ken drove back to

Philadelphia. The O'Neill had been heady stuff; with some reluctance he went back to his job.

The Women's Christian Alliance, which happened to be located across the street from Ken's office, had been mentioned to us as an agency that might have babies. It was at least worth a try. Ken said he would call. When he did, he was asked if he was white. When he said yes, he was told that the agency's babies were black and that it did not place black children with white families. Ken was startled. He saw the incident as an affront to his liberal dignity; it was the first time in his life, he said, that he had felt absolutely excluded from something because of race. Nonetheless, I sensed he was also relieved, as was I. The agency's response, however, didn't fully eliminate the possibility of adopting a black or biracial child. There were other agencies that probably would be more receptive to white couples, at least for a biracial baby. We talked around the subject, touching on it delicately every now and then. Why were we so timid?

It was true, as Ken said, that being black in the States was a political as well as an identity issue. But was that simply an excuse for us, an out? Was our concern with identity a form of racism, or a reasonable psychological concern? I thought of the "children's study" and of a baby in it. I imagined different skins, different kinds of hair. I could detect no difference in the feelings I had toward that tiny baby in the crib. But was that in itself just sentimentality on my part? Did babies really have racial identities? Not at least in the way older children and adults had.

Many blacks, for example the woman Ken spoke to at WCA, were not sure whites made good parents for black children. But, I felt, for some blacks to believe that and for us to accept it very likely implied different things. The reason Ken mentioned for not wanting to consider a black child at the moment was that his parents would find it difficult or impossible to accept. That seemed too easy to me. Was he avoiding his own feelings? Or was it simply that I didn't understand that pressure because I knew my parents, had they been alive, would have supported, probably even enthusiastically encouraged, the idea. But maybe they were just the kind of white liberals that blacks didn't want, white liberals who weren't aware of their own prejudices and limitations.

One of the things that upset me when I thought about adopting a black child was the sense of taking on for the rest of my life something so big and overwhelming: I was convinced that if I had a black child, being nonracist and converting the world would be a motivating force in my life. I would feel personally attacked by every subtle racist comment or attitude. I would be in the middle of that war. Would I, when I came right down to it, be a good mother for a black child? Would a black child—or a biracial child—do well with a mother who wanted to take on the world in his or her defense? Was there even something suspicious in my wanting to "take on the world"?

Having children via the usual route didn't force one to confront this kind of thing. It was so easy for people to say how wonderful such and such a family was—the "special" family, multiracial and so forth—and even in passing to picture becoming one themselves. I thought of all the tearjerkers on television dealing with the mythical couple whose love is great enough to transcend all boundaries and who take into their home children of every ethnic background, age, and disability, and in the process teach the community what it really means to "love." It felt different, however, if you were singled out, as I was, and told: because you have a deficiency, you are infertile, you have no choice. You must take on the role of the truly good person and fight the battle that people who are fertile can so easily avoid—without even realizing they are doing so.

Ken, in some ways, I thought, might be less reluctant to adopt a black child than I. Perhaps it was simply that he wouldn't feel quite so much that he was taking on a battle with society. At least, parents aside, I thought he worried less about other people's attitudes, had less of a problem with feeling different, an outsider, than I did.

Before the fall semester began, we decided I should call the Children's Aid Society in Philadelphia. It was an agency, we knew, that did not have white babies but did have biracial ones. When I called, I was connected with a social worker who explained that occasionally the agency had a baby who looked white but possibly had a black parent, and Children's Aid was interested in couples who wanted to adopt that kind of child. What was important for us, I said, was that our child be able to identify racially with us at least in part. The social worker seemed to understand; at least she didn't immediately interpret that as racist. It was a very complicated issue, she acknowledged. Actually, they'd had some evidence that black babies in white families had less difficulty than biracial babies in white families. Being biracial had its own set of problems. But, on the other hand, she accepted and sympathized with our interest in a biracial child. If we decided we were definitely interested, we should let her know and she would send us a preliminary application form. There would be a wait, but she thought it quite possible that eventually there would be a baby for us. It was the first time a social worker had been that confident.

In October, as my cycle progressed, in spite of myself, I didn't feel the normal bitter pessimism. My temperature had made an unusually good dive just before it rose, suggesting to me a particularly good ovulation. It had stayed clearly up, and my breasts were quite sore. I tried to avoid touching them for fear they'd be less so, but they drew me. I couldn't get their tenderness out of my mind. I didn't want to mention it to Ken; I was afraid of both his optimism and his pessimism. I went for my monthly blood test. Dan Meyer called a few days later and said he had good news. I was pregnant. How strange fate was—I was being given this baby instead of Jonathan. We could avoid all the decisions, introspection, and agony connected to adoption. I called Ken at his office. I was taken aback when I realized he was crying.

It was glorious. I'd look at women who weren't pregnant—most of the world, I suddenly realized, when just yesterday I'd thought every other woman was pregnant—and feel sad for them. I felt more powerful than men. Probably perverse, indicative of all sorts of sexist feelings, but I didn't care. I was going to enjoy this. I would have blood tests weekly. Meyer wanted to stay closely in touch with the pregnancy. In fact, he discouraged us from telling too many people right away. The first three months in particular would be risky. We decided we would even wait to tell our families, but we had to let a few close friends in Philadelphia know. I wanted to mention it in my women's group meeting.

I didn't intend to make my announcement right at the beginning of the meeting, but I couldn't keep my news in. I was pregnant, I told them; a couple of the women cried.

The meeting was at Linda's house. She promptly brought out some glasses and wine, and we all had a toast. It was wonderful.

Ken

Susan told me about the toast. It was a reaffirmation of her feminine self, the pregnancy a much-deserved reward for her years of doubt and exile. I was startled that I might actually have a biological child. It had seemed inconceivable, literally as well as figuratively. I hadn't known the extent to which I had given up. I imagined the delivery, holding the new baby. Perhaps a bit slimy and blotchy, but legally mine. No one could take him away. It amused me how protective I'd become of Susan. I was living in a sitcom, playing Desi Arnaz to Susan's Lucille Ball. Nothing must go wrong.

One worry was the dog next door. After a month of quiet, he had again begun yowling for a couple of hours in the middle of the night. Over the past year I had done everything I could think of to get him to shut up. First, I'd gone to the owners' house and tried to talk to them. I found out their phone number and, when the dog barked in the middle of the night, began calling them. I phoned the police. Finally, I tried, unsuccessfully, to organize a neighborhood petition to take the owners to court. Susan had pretty much let me fight the battle alone. She was usually able to sleep through a dog's howling an aria right under her window. But now she began to be disturbed. One morning after we'd both been kept awake most of the night, I phoned the dog's owners. I pleaded with the woman, told her my wife was pregnant, that we'd been trying for years, that the dog was keeping her awake.

Please could she take him in at night until the danger was passed. The woman was not impressed. She'd never had any trouble having kids, she told me. She didn't hear the dog bark, and, besides, barking dogs didn't cause miscarriages. Throwing the dog poisoned meat was an attractive alternative.

In spite of the dog, the pregnancy proceeded normally for the next six weeks. Then, one morning in the middle of December, Susan called me at my office. She had begun to bleed, only slightly, but there was no doubt that she was bleeding. I asked how she was feeling. She admitted she wasn't feeling quite the same as she had. Her breasts, it seemed to her, weren't quite as sore. I frequently felt somewhat at a loss as to how to interpret Susan's analyses of her body. How could symptoms be as subtle as she implied? At other times I regarded her as an oracle. I had no real contact with what was happening to my baby. Her news about the bleeding upset me. Had she been doing anything unusual? If she had felt less pregnant two days before when she'd had her last blood test, why hadn't she talked to the doctor about it? I went home and drove her to Meyer's office. Meyer examined her and concluded that the bleeding was in the normal range. Some women bled at the beginning of a pregnancy and still bore healthy children. He told us Susan should go home to bed. I was irrationally angry with her. Preparing for Christmas would be more complicated now. And I probably wouldn't even be able to persuade her not to send out Christmas cards. As I drove her home, I fumed. Susan retreated into a particularly impenetrable silence.

Once she was in bed, I started to return to work. Susan screamed from upstairs that I had goddamn better not leave. I came back to our bed and sat down beside her.

What was I doing? she asked. How could I be so cruel? Did I have any idea what she was feeling? I responded that I couldn't if she didn't tell me. She couldn't bear it. Neither could I.

When I did leave, after we talked, at least I felt calmer. The next morning when I woke, Susan was asleep. I slipped quietly out of bed. I wanted her to sleep as long as possible. I hoped the bleeding had stopped. She woke before I left. She had been up in the night several times. She thought the bleeding was lighter. She would call if there were any changes. Later that morning, she phoned me and told me that it didn't look good. I couldn't answer for a long time. "It's very sad," Susan said. Driving home, I kept hearing those words.

I picked her up and took her to Meyer's office at the hospital. There weren't enough nurses on duty that day, and Dan asked me to assist with the examination. It was somehow appropriate. Susan lay on the table, her feet in the stirrups, while I stood at her head, my hands resting on her shoulders. Meyer sat between her knees and adjusted the light. I had never been present for a gynecological examination. I felt strangely distant from the event, and yet it was a moment of unique togetherness. The doctor palpated her stomach. His face was intense. It helped to learn of the end that way, standing behind Susan, being there, even if I could not feel the pressure of the speculum and the emptiness I imagined only Susan could know. Dan stood up. "It's over," he said.

After Susan had dressed, Dan embraced her and told us how sorry he was. We went out to lunch together. At least Susan didn't need to go home and back to bed. The worst was over. There would be other times. We would have another chance.

One of the causes for depression after the miscarriage was that we again were returned to the discouraging business of thinking about adoption. We called Bronson and Korman to remind them we were still waiting. We filled out the preliminary application for Children's Aid Society. One of Susan's colleagues gave us the name of another contact at the Edna Gladney Home, a Mrs. Pinkney. This was our third try at the Gladney Home. Neither Susan nor I was optimistic about this new contact, but, of course, we had to go out and meet the woman and give it a try. Susan called her, and she enthusiastically invited us to come by—at 5:00 P.M., she said. That would give us enough time to meet her children, all of whom had been adopted through Gladney, before her husband came home. Susan got the impression that we would not be welcome once he arrived. Susan arranged to miss an afternoon meeting, and I extricated myself from my office early. We drove the hour and a quarter to Princeton, convinced we were wasting our time.

The house was a large, white mansion, set back on a lawn rolling down to the street. Three cars, one a Porsche and one a Mercedes, were in the driveway. Mrs. Pinkney ushered us into her living room, and we sat down a bit uneasily. What struck me immediately as most extraordinary, in that rather plush, aqua-colored living room, was the number of dogs, six or seven, of which no two were alike and all of which exhibited an interesting and grotesque variety of ailments. One had three legs. One, a small and long-haired Pekinese-like dog, was lying on a pillow twitching. Another had a humped back. The Quasimodos of dogdom.

Mrs. Pinkney wanted to know about us. How wonderful our careers sounded. And I was also a writer! She thought Susan, with her contacts with adolescents, could be in an excellent position to encourage girls who were pregnant to seek out the Gladney Home. It was such a good experience for them, at such a trying time in young girls' lives. But we must, she said, meet her children. She called them to come in. Blond, blue-eyed teenagers, they were on their way to or from tennis courts and were embarrassed, I thought, at being introduced as model adoptees. They quickly left. We were clearly intelligent and educated people, Mrs. Pinkney went on. One thing she was sure we wanted in children was intelligence. That was one thing that was so wonderful about Gladney. The agency matched the children to the adopting parents. Her oldest son, whom we had not met, had just begun Harvard. Surely we would want our children to be able to do that. Her husband would be coming home soon. We got up to leave. Mrs. Pinkney assured us we would be given careful attention at Gladney if we wrote and mentioned her name. Susan, in the car, said she didn't believe it. Neither did I. But we still had to write.

A letter returned promptly, thanking us for our continued interest in Gladney but saying the agency was not increasing its waiting list of adoptive parents. Susan wrote Mrs. Pinkney saying that as we'd expected, the Gladney Home had answered that it would not be able to help us. I was sure the resentment in that "as we'd expected" would be lost on her.

Popper was still a possibility. Perhaps his approach to Colombia could work. I had called him a couple of months before and had found that he had not forgotten about our interest in Colombia. He had, in fact, written a second letter to inquire about the status of things there. He now phoned to say that he had received a reply from the

Colombian lawyer and would send us a translation of the letter. The total cost of an adoption through this particular lawyer could be in excess of $8,000, $1,500 or more of which went to the Colombian attorney. Another $2,000 or more would go to Popper. We would have to pay for the care and feeding of the baby once it was born and would have to fly to Colombia. The cost seemed high, although perhaps not unduly so, since it included our travel to Colombia. Popper's bill was higher than I expected. But again the foreign connection might logically cost more.

After a month's break following her miscarriage, Susan was back on her temperature, Clomid, progesterone, blood-test regimen. Dan Meyer, fortunately, had suggested only one blood test was necessary. After her February appointment Susan reported that Meyer was recommending that all his infertility patients meet with a psychologist, Judy Gross, who was now working at the hospital. If Susan wanted to go, I hardly cared to object, although I found psychology—and psychiatry— suspect.

The psychologist greeted us at her door. I noticed she had difficulty moving across the room and sitting down. She was arthritic. I liked her. She was open, immensely supportive, and seemed impressed by us. She referred to her own arthritis as something that gave her insight into the pain of infertility. It was an odd comparison—infertility and arthritis—but Susan immediately responded to it. We talked about losing Jonathan, about Susan's miscarriages, about how much we wanted a baby. Judy spoke of envying people sitting on the grass—something so simple that everyone else took it for granted. Her sister, Judy said, had adopted a baby, now a little girl, from Colombia.

If we were interested, she was sure her sister would be glad to meet us and talk about it.

Susan suggested we invite the sister, Bonnie Klein, and her family to dinner. They came just a week later. Their little girl was rambunctious and engaging. And probably "biracial" by most U.S. stereotypes. That threw me at the beginning. Would we be taking on the political problems of a biracial child as well as the problems of a foreign adoption? Bonnie warned us we might have to wait for a baby from this Colombian agency, La Casita de Nicolás, but she guaranteed that eventually we would get one. A group of people in the area had already adopted, or were in the process of adopting, from the agency. She was having a party in several weeks for the whole Colombian group and invited us to come.

I told her about the fees for adopting through Popper and his Colombian connection. The Colombian attorney's fee was not only too high, Bonnie said, but La Casita de Nicolás would refuse to deal with a lawyer charging so much. There was something suspicious about such large amounts of money. An adoption through La Casita would cost only the lawyer's fees, usually about $300, and the cost of our getting papers together and our trip there. Our choice was obvious. We would cast our lot with La Casita.

I wrote Popper and explained that we had come up with another Colombian connection that seemed more promising and considerably cheaper. I thanked him for his help and said, in effect, that we wouldn't be needing his services. Popper immediately sent a bill for $385, $80 of which was for the initial hour we'd spent listening to his stories. I was annoyed. Susan was outraged. For her the bill was almost two weeks' full-time salary. Our experience with Bronson and the nature of our hour with Popper had led us to assume he wouldn't charge for that time. The remainder of the bill also appeared rather high for what he had done for us. Why, moreover, had he waited until this point to send us a bill? Popper fell in the category of someone attempting to make money off adoptions, albeit legally. I wrote to say that we thought the bill unfair and requested that he deduct the fee for our initial visit. He did, although he included a letter saying he felt "exploited." When I sent the money, I added a note saying "exploited" was exactly how we felt. Bad feelings on both sides.

Through Bonnie, Susan made contact with another woman, Pat Smith, who had adopted two Colombian babies. She had lunch with her and her children. That night she seemed even more committed to the Colombian route. Still, we decided not to go to Bonnie's party. Meeting many babies was hard, even for me and even if people claimed that soon we'd be bringing our own to such a gathering. On Bonnie's recommendation, Susan did call and talk to John and Carmela Alfaro, a Colombian couple living in Philadelphia who had been instrumental in many of the adoptions. Carmela said they'd be glad to help in any way they could.

The first step was to write a personal letter to La Casita de Nicolás. Pat Smith suggested that for the moment we omit mentioning we had both been divorced. Susan drafted the letter. We revised it until it was acceptable to both of us. While we were waiting for a reply from Colombia, we could start getting our papers in order. Pat gave us a list of what the agency would probably require: divorce decrees, marriage license, financial statement, doctors' certifications of health, letters from clergy, friends, and employers. From each employer we needed both a reference and a salary statement. Could those be the same letter? John Alfaro's advice was that they should not. That meant four letters right there. We would also need a "homestudy"—a report done by a social worker describing and evaluating us as potential parents. Each paper would have to be in triplicate and have to be notarized, authenticated at City Hall, and then stamped at the Colombian Consulate. I couldn't believe the need to authenticate a notarization. I'd always assumed that a notarization was the best you could do. But no! And it all cost money. That was the key. Establishing who we were was part of the point, of course, even the major part. But I still suspected that all of the formal nonsense was merely another way for Philadelphia and Colombia to make bucks. The Colombian Consulate, we learned, charged $7.50 to seal each document.

Besides the papers to go to Colombia, we needed to contact our local immigration office and start filling out forms for the baby. Eventually, a letter would also be required from the state of Pennsylvania approving us as adopting parents. For that we might need a *second* homestudy.

One paper for Colombia that concerned us was a letter from someone in the clergy. We didn't know any such person. We weren't churchgoers. Recently, however, we had made one contact. Susan had a student, Anna, who early in the semester had asked her if she knew of a Noah's Ark play for children. Anna ran the Sunday-school program at Saint Mark's, a Center City Episcopal church. Susan recommended that she get someone to write a play and offered to ask me. I met with Anna, liked her, and spent several weekends writing a play and then working with her and the children. That had been a couple of

months ago. Now we decided we should go to Saint Mark's
for a couple of months and then ask the rector to write a
letter. Perhaps marginally dishonest, but we didn't have
any other ideas. Susan rather liked going. There were
things about the service she enjoyed. It wasn't that easy
for me. I had been deeply involved in the church earlier
in my life. As an adolescent I had preached sermons in the
mountains of Virginia. I had thought of going into the
ministry. For me, leaving the church had been much
more conscious and significant than Susan's easing away
from it. Susan didn't mind saying things she didn't believe
in a church service. I did. In light of her present
equanimity I didn't understand why she earlier had been
disturbed by Holt's and Dillon's concern for the religion
of their adoptive parents. Susan responded that the
Colombian agency seemed less judgmental about religion. They certainly focused on it less. Still, she supposed
she had changed. The issue wasn't as important to her as
it had been.

It was May 1980. The school semester was nearing an
end for Susan. She assumed she should take over most of
the adoption work. I readily and somewhat guiltily ac-
quiesced. Almost every evening for weeks, I would get a
new installment on her efforts. One of the first things to
do, she reported from her discussion with Pat Smith, was
to set a homestudy in motion. An institutional homestudy
would be acceptable to Pennsylvania as well as Colombia,
whereas a free-lance one would be acceptable only to
Colombia. She talked to the Philadelphia Department of
Public Welfare, the Lutheran Children and Family Service, the Children's Aid Society, and finally the Association for Jewish Children. The last was the only one willing
to do a homestudy for people adopting through a foreign

agency. Their study would require four visits and supervision and would cost at least three hundred dollars, but they could not begin it until August. That would delay our application to Colombia until at least September. We decided to arrange for a free-lance homestudy, which could be done sooner. We would deal later with the second homestudy needed to satisfy Pennsylvania requirements. I got a recommendation of a social worker—Monica Peters. I called her. She could do the study within a few weeks.

The letter from Colombia arrived. It included a list of requirements. Much jibed with what we'd been told previously, but, Susan pointed out, it was still confusing. I thought she should talk to the friends who were advising us. What was meant, for example, by financial references? Statements from our banks and from our employers? Past income-tax forms? A summary by an accountant? Susan reported that Pat, Bonnie, John, and Carmela all had slightly different interpretations. More important, the letter from La Casita made it sound like everything—each original and both copies of it—was to be notarized, authenticated, and then sealed at the consulate. Susan checked with the consulate. The official she talked to claimed all that was necessary. Pat said it wasn't and that we shouldn't believe the consulate.

Then there was the question of getting translations. Bonnie had told us that all of our documents, with the exception of our birth and marriage certificates, should be translated into Spanish. The letter from La Casita included a sentence suggesting we get our documents translated *"si es posible,"* "if possible"—implying Bonnie was right. Pat Smith, Susan discovered, didn't agree. She felt it was safer to let La Casita handle the translations. Recently a couple she knew had had their papers translated only to have Bienestar, the official state welfare organization, insist that everything be retranslated on the grounds that it didn't know the translator. And if we did have the translations done, would they have to be in triplicate and notarized, authenticated, and sealed? It was possible we could spend hundreds of dollars on our documents alone. I suggested that we write and ask La Casita. Susan objected that La Casita was so slow in answering that we could wait months for an answer. Perhaps we'd never get one. Her impression was that 90 percent of the time La Casita was relatively relaxed about the documents, at least more so than she. What unsettled her, she complained, was the knowledge that periodically they were sticklers about something and there was no way to anticipate what it would be. Bureaucratic details took on emotional weight. She couldn't bear anything going wrong. In the end, I won on this one. We wouldn't translate the documents but would include a note saying that we would be glad to do so. Susan was as preoccupied with gathering papers as with following her temperature, Clomid, progesterone routine. I felt a bit guilty, though, spared as I was this mundane, tedious aspect of adopting.

We actually had a deadline now. John and Carmela had offered to take our packet of documents in person to Medellín when they went to Colombia in the middle of July. Susan sent off for my birth and divorce decrees and for her own birth certificate. She found that her certificate and her twin sister's were mixed up. She went to City Hall for her divorce decree and our marriage certificate. Everything took longer than she anticipated. We decided which friends we should ask for recommendations. Susan called them. She asked her boss for a letter, and I, mine.

She got statements from the two banks where we had accounts. Dan Meyer wrote a letter both recommending us and verifying Susan's good health.

Immigration sent us the necessary forms, and we met downtown to have fingerprints taken. These would not be needed until later. But it took a couple of months for prints to be processed, and it was possible they wouldn't be successful the first time. Pat Smith had tried three times before hers were accepted. It was necessary to get the ball rolling.

The next thing to do was to arrange for a meeting with the rector at Saint Mark's Church to ask for a recommendation. I no longer felt uncomfortable about the request. Gradually, over the last months, I had found myself attracted again to the church, moved in a way I'd not expected. I indicated to the rector at our meeting that I wanted to follow my religious feelings further. Susan was shocked. I felt it had little to do with her. Becoming religious, Susan responded, was a major event and she wasn't prepared for that happening to me. She had assumed that we shared the same attitude toward religion. Either she hadn't known me or I had changed radically. Either way, she found it threatening. But we both agreed that the way I "rediscovered religion," as she put it, was ironic. Here we were simply trying to go through the motions so that we could get the necessary recommendation. "God works in mysterious ways," I said. "Nonsense," Susan replied.

We had trepidations about the homestudy. We were about to be judged by someone we didn't know on grounds that were unclear. We had heard of social workers snooping into closets. If we had taken custody of Jonathan, the city would have required a homestudy. We had asked Mrs. Reed what it would be like. She suggested it might be best if we "removed" our cats beforehand. Monica Peters was not what I had expected. She seemed to want us to like her as much as we wanted her to like us. She offered to send us a draft of her report. We should feel free to change things if they didn't seem accurate. She had her own supply of homestudy horror stories. Unofficial directives to disqualify people if they had chrome furniture, or a house without a basement, or were clergy. She didn't poke into closets, though Susan had cleaned them out. She was enamored of the two cats. At the end of the interview, I felt we had it cinched, in a sense. She sent us her first draft. It was very sympathetic, but some of the phrasing and a few misplaced words gave a different impression than the one we assumed Monica intended. Susan returned the draft with suggestions. Monica integrated them all. She wanted to do well by us.

Carmela suggested in one of her phone conversations with Susan that she and John help us fill out the application to accompany our papers. She thought it should be in Spanish. Susan and I felt that would be a good opportunity for us to meet. Susan invited them to dinner. John and Carmela were not officially interviewing us. Nonetheless, we would be on display, at least for a while. Just before they were due, Susan rushed out to pick up the inevitable trash on the sidewalk.

What I first noticed was that Carmela was a strikingly beautiful woman. She and John were wealthy Colombians, who owned a farm in the Colombian mountains, and a house in Philadelphia. John was South American representative for Sun Oil. They lived in a different world from ours. Yet they seemed remarkably comfortable, in spite of their rather formal dress, in our hot, un-air-conditioned house on busy Germantown Avenue with the trolleys rattling by right outside the dining-room windows. Carmela exclaimed over the house, the flowers, the garden. John was also an enthusiast, if in a different vein. He launched into a story of flying down to Colombia in a small plane, with one of his sons, slipping over the mountains on the long flight from Miami. The adventure and even the danger of it obviously delighted him.

After eating, we worked on the application at the dinner table. Filling out the form in Spanish would at least be a symbol of our willingness to do as much as we could. I wished I knew Spanish. The application asked for a physical description of each spouse: hair, eyes, skin, complexion, as well as height and weight. Carmela and John argued over what words should be used to describe us. What fine distinctions Colombians made in describing color. When John and Carmela finally agreed on what words to use, those they had chosen to describe me were entirely different from those to describe Susan. We both had brown eyes, but even our eyes were not called the same. For me: hair—*entrecano;* eyes—*oscuros;* skin—*trigueña;* complexion—*moreno.* For Susan: hair—*castaño claro;* eyes—*carmelitos;* skin—*blanca;* complexion—*blanca.*

We had only three days left before Carmela and John were leaving for Colombia. With the application form completed, there were only a couple of additional things to do—before, of course, the process of notarizing, authenticating, and sealing the documents. One was getting a statement of health from my doctor. I was to pick up the document at the doctor's office in the morning on my way to work. My boss, however, refused to postpone a meeting for a half hour. So I had to go directly to my office. Then the doctor's secretary refused to try to put the paper in the mail that day. I called back, only to have a message relayed to me from the doctor that it had been mailed the day before. That didn't seem possible, so I tracked down a secretary who could answer a few more questions. They were confused, I found, as to what letter I was talking about. Eventually, I had to make another trip across town, at rush hour, to the doctor's office. Everyone became rigid, and even a little crazy, just when I needed flexibility and sanity. At times I had been sure that getting the papers together could not be as complicated as Susan indicated. I had trouble believing that it took so much time, so much energy, to gather a portfolio of basic documents about our lives. My experience getting my health statement gave me more sympathy for her complaints.

Finally, we borrowed a Polaroid from a friend and took pictures of each other in the backyard beside one of the rosebushes. I came out looking unusually swarthy. If La Casita was concerned with matching our color with that of a child, maybe Susan's fairness would make it harder for us. My looking darker was a good thing, a good sign. We took pictures of the house. The front and the back, the dining room, the "children's study," which would be, in the future, the baby's room.

It was amazing how many papers were necessary to establish a certain kind of truth. How difficult it was for bureaucrats to imagine what Susan and I were like. The only way to define us was to collect verifiable information. Still, there was something impressively solid about the final set of documents with their stamps and seals. If anyone ever doubted our existence, this should convince them otherwise. We dropped off the packet at John and Carmela's house.

The next week Susan and I left for our 1980 vacation

in Rhode Island. There seemed even more children on the beach this summer than the year before. Maybe it was just that last summer the O'Neill had preoccupied me. This vacation I would work on a draft of a new play.

When we returned to Philadelphia two weeks later, we found a note from Carmela in the pile of mail. She wrote that she had delivered our papers. We should send La Casita some pictures of our house and a copy of our latest income-tax return. She added that there might be a problem with the homestudy. Susan again leapt into action. We had already included pictures of the house with our documents, so she assumed we needn't worry about that. We would send a copy of our income-tax form. But did it need to be in triplicate? And did it need to be notarized, authenticated, and sealed? The biggest question was about the homestudy. If it wasn't acceptable, did that mean that our papers would be held up until we sent a new one? Or would La Casita go ahead and start processing our papers and application? And what exactly was the problem with our homestudy? Monica had included her education credentials but not a description of her job at Temple University. Susan concluded that perhaps La Casita didn't know she was employed as a social worker. That sounded possible. Susan called Monica and asked her to send La Casita a description of the program in which she worked. We received a copy. There was no cover letter. Our names were never mentioned. It was unlikely La Casita would know why or for whose file it had been sent. Susan wrote La Casita about it. She also sent three copies of our last year's income-tax form. Following my suggestion, they weren't notarized, authenticated, or sealed, but a note was enclosed saying we'd be glad to do so if necessary.

Late in August Carmela returned from Colombia. She reported on the story of the homestudy. It appeared La Casita was afraid that Bienestar wouldn't accept the study because the social worker was employed by the same university as I. Temple University employed ten thousand people! Carmela said she knew that, but Bienestar didn't. La Casita was trying to play it safe. I had to admit, rewriting Monica's report had made it feel bogus. Having it turned down seemed like a kind of poetic justice.

Susan immediately renewed her efforts to get another homestudy. We assumed we could turn to the Association for Jewish Children. When Susan called, however, she was told that the agency had just changed its policy. It was now restricted to doing homestudies for Jews only. The social worker, sympathetic to our problems, recommended the Lutheran Children and Family Service. She had heard just recently that they had changed their policy. Susan immediately called the Lutherans. She phoned me at work with the news. The information about the Lutherans was accurate. The decision to begin that service had, in fact, just been made, and there wasn't even a waiting list.

First, there would be an appointment at the Lutherans' offices with one of the social workers. Then she would make a home visit. This would be an "official" homestudy. What would we have to prove about ourselves? How honest should we be? Honesty implied trusting someone we didn't know but who had a remarkable amount of power over our lives.

The first appointment was largely informational. The fee for the homestudy was to be three hundred dollars. The social worker gave us an application and personal-reference forms that we were to pass on to several friends.

They were to return them directly to her. We both needed recent physicals. That meant I would have to have a new one. We should give her divorce and marriage verification and a letter from our rector, and fill out and have witnessed a form authorizing the agency to obtain information about us. We needed police clearance. (Police clearance?) And, finally, we were each to write a short autobiography.

Susan assembled our papers and got the recommendation forms to our friends. She asked Dan Meyer to write a new letter about her health. I had a new physical. I checked into getting police clearance. We both needed new fingerprints. Once that was done, the files of the Philadelphia Police Department's Identification Unit, Detective Bureau, and Criminal Records Section were searched. We received cards stamped "No record." Finally, we wrote our autobiographies.

I resented, as much as Susan, the notion of being judged that a homestudy implied. It qualified our status as adults. But we would do as we were told. We would play the game right. The social worker arrived on her official visit. We settled ourselves in the living room. The questions she asked were not easy. How did we see ourselves as individuals, as a couple? What were we like growing up? Why had we both been previously married and divorced? What kind of child did we want and why? What were our relations like with our parents when we were growing up and now? Why did we live in the city? Why had we chosen our particular careers? She was not judgmental. I found myself being honest. Yes, I hadn't wanted children in my first marriage, but I'd become aware that was a comment on that marriage, not on my feelings about children. Susan was being honest, too, even going overboard, I thought, in stressing how much she hated school as a child. How introspective, analytical, self-conscious, the whole business made us feel. The social worker left after a couple of hours. I was quite sure she thought we were reasonable people. We put together the new packet to be mailed to Colombia. Susan had our second homestudy notarized, authenticated, and sealed. She wrote a letter describing the social worker's position, asking if we should send money at this point to cover the translation of our documents and reminding La Casita to send us a power-of-attorney form. She added (threatened?) that we would call in a month if we hadn't heard anything by then. Her excuse was that we knew the mails could be undependable. She ended by saying we were trying very hard not to be the stereotypical anxious prospective parents. I noted that we weren't succeeding very well. The next step, of course, was to wait.

Four

❧ Nicholas

Susan The summer of 1980 ended; the school semester began. I wondered if at seventy I'd wake up in the middle of the night thinking that I'd forgotten something—my Clomid? my progesterone?—or reminding myself to take a progesterone suppository with me in the morning. The fact that taking the medication had become second nature at times added to the difficulty. An hour after taking the progesterone or Clomid I'd be unable to remember whether I'd done so. Life could be much worse. I loved my teaching, my friends, Ken. But the emptiness of not having a child undercut everything. How different it had been in the beginning, when my desire to have a child—my hope that I was pregnant—had been a sustaining secret.

I still felt uncomfortable with, even betrayed by, Ken's attraction to the church. I tried, halfheartedly, to be a part of it. Ken was asked by Saint Mark's to write another children's play to be produced in early December—this one in honor of Saint Nicholas. Ostensibly, the play, *In the*

113

Nick of Time, was a retelling of a story in which that patron saint of the young rescues a boatload of children lost at sea. In reality, it was a story about a story that will not behave. A storm refuses to appear at the right time. A dragon arrives instead. The wrong hero, Saint George, turns up and mistakes a pillar for the dragon. In the end, Nicholas, unaided by the storyteller, saves the day by some fast improvisation. The Renaissance play I had directed in Virginia had given Ken the idea of a storyteller whose tale does not unfold as she intends. I played the storyteller.

A few days after the play, I went to my monthly gynecological appointment. I tried to prepare myself for the blood test and for the negative result. The blood was taken, and Dan Meyer examined me. I thought I could read in his manner the tentative knowledge that the test would not be positive. It was a normal enough appointment, except that Meyer seemed unusually rushed. As he left the examining room, he added that there was something he wanted to tell me about, but he had an emergency elsewhere. He had just had time to squeeze in my exam. The resident would talk to me. Dr. Boger came in. Another physician in the hospital was about to deliver a baby for a young Thai girl who wanted to place the child for adoption. Would my husband and I be interested in the baby? I told him I would talk to Ken and call the next morning—but even as I said that, I knew our answer would be yes. It was a big decision, I felt it necessary to add, to take a child who was so obviously of a different racial background. He was Jewish and his wife was Catholic, Dr. Boger responded; their children were similarly going to be different from their parents. I said I didn't think that was quite the same. Sure it was, he told me.

Anyway, Ken and I should let them know as soon as possible. And he stepped out of the room.

I tried to move as though nothing had happened, but the world had stopped. I went into the bathroom off the examining room, locked the door, and wept—and couldn't understand why. Once in my car, I realized I wasn't ready to go home or to call Ken. I drove past the Philadelphia Museum of Art, saw the sign announcing a Noguchi sculpture exhibit, and on an impulse decided to stop and see it. One room was almost completely filled with models of plans Noguchi had made for playgrounds. I forced myself to focus on them. They were wonderfully molded and, at least as models, suggested surfaces and forms that encouraged both play and security. I wondered what it would feel like to be in them. How complicated it was to make a playground safe. Most of the playgrounds in the exhibit had never been constructed. How depressing for Noguchi, I thought. Here the models themselves were being treated like works of art, but did they really exist if they lived only in the form of an idea, a plan? A dream without the reality felt empty. And playgrounds seemed important in a way they'd never been before.

I read the biographical statements and wandered through the rest of the exhibit—the stage and costume designs and his weighted, yet floating, sculptures. Noguchi was Japanese-American. He had been living in California when Pearl Harbor was attacked, and though he initially had "escaped" from the West Coast, he later found himself interned in a relocation camp for Japanese-Americans. How would it feel to be a citizen of one country, to feel a part of that country yet be considered an enemy by it? How would it feel to be a minority—and visibly, physically different—from the group in power?

I remembered the evening my first husband-to-be and I had told his parents we were thinking of getting engaged. The Zeitlins had not supported the idea. They were Jewish and I was not. Did I fully understand what it would be like to be a Gentile married to a Jew in this society? The evening had ended on a wary note. It had always moved me that once I was actually engaged, the Zeitlins accepted me as a daughter. And when my marriage broke up, they had told me that they did not want to lose me. Now as I walked through the Noguchi exhibit, I suddenly understood, in terms of this new baby, what the Zeitlins were feeling that night. Felt from the inside, this baby would be of my blood and Ken's blood, but from the outside he or she would be seen to be different—in a society in which differences mattered. How painful would that discrepancy be? At the moment it felt agonizing. A couple of hours had passed. It was time to go home.

It occurred to me as I was driving that I really didn't know much about the baby. When I got home, I called the doctor's office and asked to speak to Dr. Boger. There had been some confusion in the message he'd been given, he told me. The pregnant girl was not Thai; she was from Taiwan, from Taipei. The biological father was also Chinese. The girl had recently—within the last couple of months—come from China with her mother. She was only about fourteen. As far as he knew, she was healthy and there'd been no problems with the pregnancy.

Ken arrived home at his usual time, and I gave him the news. He was shocked that I hadn't called him. What had I been thinking of? This was great news. We just had to discuss it rationally and carefully. How can decisions of this sort be rational? I responded. There he was, forcing something that was hardly rational into an intellectual mold and in the process totally avoiding the whole issue. I was the one, he complained, who was doing a pretty good job of avoiding the issue. I was the one who hadn't called him to tell him the news. Why? Did I think it didn't matter to him? It would be his baby as much as mine. We had said we'd be willing to try another private adoption. Otherwise, why were we still in touch with Korman and Bronson? And we'd also talked about adopting a Korean child. This opportunity was right in line with what we'd been thinking. That was just my point, I continued: he knew as well as I that we would take this baby. We were far from rationally moving through a discussion to a decision. The decision was a foregone conclusion. It didn't matter what I was feeling. It was totally superfluous. What on earth was I talking about? he cried. Of course it mattered how I felt. We were in this together. He wasn't assuming anything! Oh, wasn't he? I said sarcastically. I was always the one who didn't see things rationally. Why wouldn't he acknowledge that what we were contemplating was frightening?

What were we fighting about? I put my head down on my arms. I felt Ken move and looked in time to see him seize a wooden kitchen chair we'd recently bought, raise it above his head, and smash it to the floor. The legs shattered. He had never before in a fight done anything physically destructive. There was a moment of silence. Then— why, I exclaimed, did he have to choose a good chair? There was a decrepit, ugly kitchen chair right next to it. Why couldn't he have broken that one? Aesthetic judgments, he responded, hardly seemed appropriate at such a moment. He even appeared a little pleased with himself.

Somehow I felt calmer. We both acknowledged we

wanted the baby. To have a newborn would be fantastic fortune. We would just have to be sure we didn't assume the baby was ours. We couldn't make the same mistake we'd made with Jonathan. It was something we would have to keep in our minds at all times. The other issue, the fact that the baby would be Chinese, was something about which we could talk to people. Dr. Boger had missed the point. His children shared their parents' racial background. Our baby would not. Ken suggested calling one of my colleagues, Lily Yeh. I phoned. We had a good chance, I told her, of adopting a Chinese baby. What did she think about that? "That's wonderful!" Lily cried; "Chinese babies are *so* beautiful!" That wasn't quite our worry, I told her. We had lots of questions. How would the Chinese community feel about a Chinese baby having Caucasian parents? Being Chinese didn't at the moment have the political identity that being black had in the States, but was it possible that in the next ten years it would become a political issue? Didn't we know, Lily laughed, that the Chinese were going to take over the world? It would be very helpful for us to have a Chinese son. "But seriously," she continued in her lilting Chinese voice, "the real bond is the human one, isn't it? In light of that, racial differences are unimportant, don't you think?"

Asking Lily her reaction was a rigged question. She was Chinese, and her Chinese roots were strong, but she had married a Caucasian and had a son by him. I thought of another rigged call. One of my colleagues, Terri Conn, had three biological Caucasian children and an adopted Korean daughter. I phoned her and told her our news. Was Jenny ever made to feel like an outsider at school? How did she react to being different? Terri answered that so far as she could tell, Jenny wasn't bothered by her differentness; she seemed to enjoy it. When she'd been told to eat her vegetables a couple of nights earlier, she'd announced firmly to her parents that Korean people did not like brussels sprouts. A couple of years before, she had become an American citizen. As the time drew near, she'd seemed unexpectedly upset about the idea of being "naturalized." Finally, they discovered what the problem was. She assumed that after the ceremony she would look like her brothers and sister, and, she told her parents, she *liked* her almond eyes and skin. She wanted to keep them.

Ken and I hadn't talked at all about the Colombia adoption. Would this hurt our chances with the agency there? La Casita would give us a second baby once it had given us the first. If we took this baby, would that make us ineligible for one in Colombia? And would that make it impossible to get a second child? Ken thought it was a mistake to think about a second baby before we had the first; one was all he could deal with. But, I worried, what if we lost this baby as we had Jonathan? Might we be left with no child at all? Ken suggested we talk to Pat Smith. She was excited by our news and thought we would be crazy to pass up this chance. "For the moment," she continued, "why mention anything at all to La Casita?" Carmela and John, she was sure, would agree.

The chair still lay shattered on the kitchen floor. The next morning, Ken called a carpenter, who said he would come and take a look at it. Perhaps he could make some new spindles and reglue it. Then, with Ken standing at my shoulder, I called Dan Meyer's office and left a message with the receptionist that Ken and I wanted the baby. Ken took the morning off, and we waited for the return call.

Ken

The phone rang and I answered it. It was Dan Meyer. He warned that we had to act quickly.

The child might be delivered as early as Christmas—a week and a half away. He could give us a few more details. The girl and her mother came from a middle-class background. The girl had plans to go to college. (Jonathan's birth mother, I reminded myself, had also wanted to go to college.) They had left Taiwan after the untimely death of the girl's father and were eager to establish themselves in their new country. The precariousness of their economic situation wouldn't make that easy and certainly was one reason they wanted the baby to be adopted. More important, in the Chinese community an illegitimate baby would not be readily accepted. In fact, the pregnancy had been kept a secret, and the biological grandmother had asked that the baby go to a Caucasian couple, preferably an educated one, and one in the Philadelphia area. She and her daughter were going to settle in Boston near relatives as soon as the baby was born. She wanted the relatively simple, private, and independent arrangement that a nonagency adoption would allow. The first thing for us to do was to call a lawyer to act as an intermediary.

We might have a baby by Christmas! We had a great deal to do. It was the end-of-the-semester crunch for Susan. She had yet to give her exams, correct them, and hand in final grades. As usual, we had done little Christmas shopping. We were due to leave for Massachusetts, to spend Christmas with Susan's family, in exactly nine days. And, as always before I left on vacation, I had projects at my office that I had to complete—a grant proposal to write, several readers of manuscripts to track down, and papers to prepare for an early January meeting.

I called Bronson to ask if he would handle the adoption. His secretary said that he had gone to Europe. He would not be back in the office for a month. Suddenly, we had no lawyer to turn to. I called Meyer back. Dan recommended that we talk to a nurse he knew who had recently adopted a child privately. She told me about a lawyer, Nathan Berger, who with his wife, Celeste, handled her adoption. He had, in fact, placed more children privately than anyone else in Philadelphia. I left a message at their office saying we were interested in adopting a baby and wanted Mr. Berger to act as our lawyer. Celeste Berger returned my call late that afternoon. No, she told me, there were no babies available. So they couldn't be of help to couples wanting to find and adopt a child. This was different, I said. We *had* a baby. We just needed a lawyer. Celeste immediately set up an appointment for Monday.

Our meeting was not with Nat but with Celeste, who we learned would handle most of the preliminary details. She was a paralegal, trained in the procedures of private adoptions. She began by warning us how risky such adoptions were. We had lost a baby, Susan told her, and we went on to tell her about Jonathan. So then you know, said Celeste. Susan hurriedly added that this seemed a much better bet. This girl and her mother were not in a position to take care of a new baby. "Nothing," said Celeste, "is ever sure until it's over." Her matter-of-factness was a little appalling. I reminded myself that we needed someone who wouldn't allow us to think of the baby as ours until he really was.

We should note carefully the following steps and procedures, Celeste began. I pulled out a pen and paper. She would contact the girl and her mother, she continued, and get back in touch with us. The first thing we should

do was get the name of a pediatrician from Susan's gyne-
cologist. We should contact him and tell him about the
Bergers and the adoption and that we would be in touch
with him when the child was born. We should also let him
know what physical matters, such as circumcision, were
important to us. Celeste would supply a list of things for
us to buy for the baby to come home in. Everything had
to be new. When the pediatrician called the obstetrician
after the baby's birth, he was not to disclose our names or
his name. He should identify the child simply as the baby
Mr. Berger was handling for adoption. There must be *no*
names. After the birth, we would need to sign a "Report
of Child Intended to Be Adopted." That would be filed
with the court. Sometime after thirty days, the biological
mother would appear in court and affirm that she was
giving up parental rights. We as adopting parents would
not appear or be involved in that proceeding. That hearing would be called the Voluntary Relinquishment. The
biological mother would have, technically, at least six
months to change her mind, though after the Voluntary
Relinquishment we would be in a relatively secure position. We would have two visits from a social worker from
the court. We should file a petition of adoption as early as
possible, three months after custody. Then anytime after
six months a hearing would be scheduled. There could be
as much as an eleven-month wait. After the Final Adoption Decree, a new birth certificate would be issued by
the Bureau of Vital Statistics in Newcastle, Pennsylvania.
The Bergers' fee would be seven hundred dollars, unless
the adoption fell through. Then there would be no
charge. The medical expenses would be in the vicinity of
three thousand dollars. Those expenses should be paid by
check to Nathan Berger. On the check should be written

"Medical Expenses Only." We would pay half of the expenses if we decided not to take the baby because of major physical problems or even death. Finally, we should note that the Bergers were the official intermediaries on all records.

I believed the Bergers were a lucky find. They knew and had worked with the right people in the public-welfare system and in the family court. Celeste's lack of optimism was good for us. At least, said Susan, it was different from the attitude of the lawyer who had handled Jonathan. And we wanted, after all, everything to be different this time.

Time was important because the birth was impending and also because the Bergers planned to spend the Christmas holidays in the Caribbean. Everything had to be arranged, if possible, before they left. It was entirely possible that they would be out of the country at the time of the birth. And, of course, Susan and I were also planning to travel during the holidays—not only to visit Susan's family in Massachusetts, but also mine in northern Virginia. In between those trips, I had to be at a conference in New York City. Not being at home, waiting by the telephone, made us both nervous. I was easier to reach at my office the last week before Christmas than Susan. We left my office as the primary number.

Two days later, Celeste called me to say that she was uneasy. Despite her efforts to contact the girl's mother, she had made no headway. The woman had not returned her calls. She worried about the strength of the grandmother's commitment to the adoption. Our experience with Jonathan weighed on my mind. The birth grandmother's agreement to the procedure would be critical. Her daughter, after all, was a fourteen-year-old minor.

I phoned Susan at home. What should we do? Perhaps Dan Meyer should check it out. We had to know where things stood. This limbo was agony. I called and reached Dan. He said he was quite certain the girl's mother had not changed her mind about the adoption, but he would contact the attending physician to find out if anything had gone wrong. Later that day he called to say that the woman was difficult to reach because of the odd hours of her job. He was sure that she would be in touch with the Bergers soon.

A meeting did occur between Celeste and the birth relatives three days before Susan and I were scheduled to leave town for Christmas. Celeste phoned us afterward and said she was reassured by their attitude. That Celeste used the word "reassured" made us almost euphoric. We had to work on controlling our expectations. There was another problem, however. The girl had been accompanied by her mother and an aunt who was down from Boston. Only the aunt spoke English. That meant that all of the documents would have to be translated into Chinese, and the girl's mother wanted the aunt to do the translations. She did not want Celeste to arrange a professional translation because she wanted to prevent the community's learning about the baby. There seemed to be no getting around the fear. Although there was no legal objection to her doing the translation, Celeste worried that her English would not be up to the job and that the subsequent documents would be faulty. She and Nat had dealt previously, however, with a similar case that had worked out. (Score one, I thought, for working with people experienced in adoption.)

The birth grandmother had also hired a lawyer, which the Bergers thought unusual. Susan, however, argued that was a good sign. The girl's mother seemed to want the adoption to be official. She and her daughter were not acting on a whim. Now that the Bergers had contacted the birth relatives, I could take the next step, as directed by Celeste. I talked to the neonatologist who would be acting as the baby's pediatrician. All was set there.

Susan's women's group had a meeting. Susan didn't want to go. She didn't want to say anything about the baby. Telling people about Jonathan, she told me, had helped jinx it. When she came home, she said it had been a dreadful meeting. People assumed she was depressed and kept pushing her to talk. She shouldn't have gone.

I got my office work in order so that I could leave for the holiday. Susan corrected her papers and handed in her grades. We finished our Christmas shopping and even went to the yearly Christmas parties. Only a very few friends in Philadelphia knew of our extraordinary emotional state. The day before Christmas, we drove to Massachusetts. We took with us the name and number of the hotel at which the Bergers would be staying in the Bahamas. The Bergers had our holiday itinerary. Susan had plotted our movements practically to the hour.

We had to tell our families something. We might get a call about the baby's birth any hour. Like Susan, however, I didn't want to discuss the baby until he or she was an accomplished fact. After dinner on Christmas Eve, Debby's son, David, went to bed, and the adults lingered at the dining-room table. It was time. Susan told them. We might be adopting a baby due to be born any day. The baby would be Chinese. And we didn't want to talk about it anymore. There was a surprised silence. Aunt Doris murmured that it was just wonderful. From then on, every time the telephone rang, everyone froze. Perhaps we would have a Christmas baby, but December 25 came and went, leaving behind only the traditional gifts.

After my business in New York we went to visit my parents and sisters. There I made the same cautious announcement as Susan had in Massachusetts. There was the same weighted but silent response. On New Year's Day, back home again, we hosted what had become a traditional brunch for a few friends, telling no one of our 1981 New Year's wish.

We were worried, of course, that something had gone awry, that the lack of news was an indication of a new and fatal twist of the knife. Celeste contacted us when she and her husband returned to the city. They had been in touch with the obstetrician, who said only that the girl was due to deliver any day. Possibly, he said, he had been mistaken about the date. The language barrier made it difficult to be precise about conception. Further, there was some confusion about how she had gotten pregnant in the first place. The girl's mother claimed that her daughter had been raped by an unknown man. The girl had spoken of a boyfriend, someone nearly her age, a family acquaintance. I was quite sure, as was Susan, that the girl's story was the correct one. I asked about the two other babies Celeste had said she and her husband were involved in placing. One of the babies, Celeste told me, was in fact born on Christmas Day. The biological mother had interpreted that birth date as a sign she should keep the baby.

Despite our experience with Jonathan, and our vow never to identify with the birth parents of a child, Susan and I allowed ourselves to speculate on the girl and her mother. What were they like? How were they coping with this difficult time in their lives? They seemed far away, literally and figuratively foreign—yet profoundly woven into the fabric of our lives. The girl's mother was clearly a woman of great strength, I decided. Because we had lost Jonathan to his birth grandmother, I found myself focusing on this unknown woman, speculating constantly about her motivations, aspirations, honesty. Did Susan realize, I asked her one day, that the girl's mother could be as young as we were, even younger? Suddenly she was a grandmother in name only, and her youth made her more threatening. She could easily manage to raise an infant. She was young enough to bear one herself. Such ruminations were deadly, of course. We tried to work on avoiding them.

Susan asked Peshe to buy the baby things Celeste said she needed to take to the hospital. The list was precise. Celeste believed firmly that the price tags should still be on everything when the baby was picked up. The reason, she said, was simple. The adopting parents must convey to the biological relatives and to the hospital that they would supply their child with the newest and the best. Peshe was amused by the requirements. New equaled best? Was a plastic carrying bag really necessary? An undershirt, a nightgown, a sweater, a receiving blanket, *and* a bunting? Susan told her to follow the directions exactly. Peshe dropped off her purchases the next day. Everything was yellow or white—appropriate for a boy or girl. She had done everything as told. The next morning, Susan delivered the bundle to the Bergers. To her great relief, she told me that evening, Celeste accepted the package without looking at what it contained. She didn't know if she could have endured seeing the contents a second time.

The girl's aunt, meanwhile, back in Boston, was proceeding with the translations slowly. Celeste had been on the phone with her several times. Once again, she mentioned to us that she was concerned whether the aunt was really doing the translations correctly. She didn't like not being able to meet with her. The girl's mother, also, was pressuring Celeste to ask us to pay for her lawyer and to compensate the aunt for her time spent translating the documents. Celeste was adamant. We were to pay for all medical expenses, for our own lawyer, and for court costs, but that was all. Susan worried that Celeste was being too rigid. After all, what was important was for us to get the baby. But I argued that Celeste knew what she was doing. To pay for anything more than she was allowing would open the door to quasi-illegal bartering. We began worrying, however, that the birth grandmother might want to sell the baby, which was what I had conjectured had happened to Jonathan. Did the girl's mother know, we wondered, that she could get thousands of dollars on the black market? On the other hand, middle-class people, recently arrived in the United States, who wanted to make a home for themselves here, surely would not be interested in dabbling in something illegal. Perhaps the girl's mother simply did not trust us. She was new in the country. She and her daughter must be going through a traumatic period. She must be feeling vulnerable herself. If only she could know that there was no way we would fail to keep our part of the bargain. We were more than willing to pay every cent of the medical expenses. Even the TV in the private hospital room.

We knew the financial ropes from our experience with Jonathan. We had to give the hospital a deposit for the girl's room in advance of delivery. That, it turned out, came to fifteen hundred dollars in cash. Blue Cross/Blue Shield, as before, would not cover such expenses. The rest, another fifteen hundred dollars, would have to be paid at the time we received the baby. The danger in such an arrangement was that an unscrupulous person could give birth to a child she had promised could be adopted and then reclaim custody some time after leaving the hospital—ending up with a baby and a cheap vacation in the most expensive hotel room in town.

After New Year's Day, I went back to work. Susan was on semester break. She threw her energies into writing an article. I worked on my new play. If the baby came, we would have no more time to write. We could not allow ourselves to prepare in any explicit way for the baby. Last time in spite of our efforts we had prepared too much. This time we wouldn't even buy formula.

One evening, we visited John and Carmela and delivered to them the power-of-attorney form needed for the adoption procedure in Colombia. The Alfaros were about to go to Medellín for an extended visit and had offered to check on the progress of our petition there. We both liked acting in a way that did not seem consistent with the arrival into our home, possibly in just a few days, of a newborn baby. We discussed with the Alfaros what we should tell La Casita. Our application to La Casita stated that we had no children. If we acquired one, should we change the application? Would having one child mean we'd have to have a new homestudy? We didn't want to jeopardize our chances in Colombia. Nor did we want to put ourselves in the position of lying. Carmela felt La Casita would be pleased that the baby it would give us would have a brother or sister. She didn't believe our chances would be hurt. Most American agencies, however, felt differently. Children had to be two to three years apart. And even Carmela acknowledged that, for the moment, there was no need to say anything. After all, the child was not even born yet. And once it was born, there would be a period of at least six months in which we would be legally no more than foster parents. Practically speaking, we would be foolish to raise the subject with La Casita before the issuance of a final decree.

Another evening, we decided to see a film, and I pushed for *Kramer vs. Kramer,* a story of a custody battle between an estranged husband and wife. Choosing it was probably a form of masochism, but I was drawn to it precisely because it was about a custody battle—not an adoption one, but close enough. After the film, we went to a favorite bar in the city to have a drink. We speculated whether this time out would be our last "date" as a childless couple. We drank to the possibility.

The gourmet group was scheduled for a dinner on January 13. Joe-Blume, the group's official secretary, had called and cleared that date with us just before we left for Massachusetts in December. Susan had told him that was good for us. We felt we had to assume we wouldn't have the baby. Now we were glad of that decision. The dinner was Middle Eastern. A man in the group who was an architect prepared the main dish—a rack of lamb. It had the presence of an architectural creation. Had anyone, he asked, seen the Noguchi exhibit? He thought it was wonderful—Noguchi was an architect's sculptor. Susan had seen it, I commented. I couldn't look at her. Our secret was too powerful. We ate and drank to excess in that Center City townhouse located just across the street from the Kleins, the couple who had first put us in touch with La Casita de Nicolás.

The translation of necessary documents had proceeded during the early weeks of January. We fought back the hope that everything would work out. We told ourselves that this time next year we would be going to movies, cooking together, and, if Susan were not on progesterone, sleeping late on weekends. As the days rolled on, Celeste became more relaxed about the birth grandmother's attitude and the translations. We became, if anything, more anxious. The Bergers were going off on another vacation. We were concerned about that. What would happen if the baby were born during that time? I called Nat to find out how they planned to handle the situation. The conversation was not satisfactory. Nat was evasive, cool. Susan was distraught. We had to have some kind of legal coverage! If the baby were born and the Bergers were out of town, the biological grandmother and mother could think the adoption had fallen through. We would be helpless. Maybe we should look for another lawyer. I felt it was too late to do that. How could I stand there and say we could do nothing? cried Susan. What could she suggest we do? I was trembling. One thing for sure, this was the last private adoption we would try.

Later that day, we understood Nat's evasiveness. The girl was in labor when I called. She delivered a son weighing seven pounds two ounces. He was healthy and beautiful. The girl was placed in a private room. The baby was put in the nursery. Most likely, she never saw him. A nurse we knew described the biological mother to us. An unusually lovely young girl, watching cartoons, with a stuffed animal in the bed beside her.

The next day I talked to Dan Meyer, who relayed a message from the neonatologist. The baby was in excellent shape. That same morning Susan had to decide whether to begin her cycle of Clomid and progesterone. We talked about it. It was not a hard decision. Perhaps pretending that there was no baby out there across the city would bring him to us.

The delivery had been by cesarean section, which meant that the girl would have to stay in the hospital a few extra days. That meant a higher hospital bill. It also meant a delay in our taking custody of the baby. Usually, the child did not leave the hospital in adoption cases until the mother left. At one point, Celeste thought that the hospital would agree to release the baby ahead of the birth mother. Then there was evidence of jaundice. The release would have to be delayed until that cleared up. While the baby basked under a bilirubin lamp, we went through the motions of living—mechanically eating, sleeping, working, filling our heads with junk television and our hands with busywork. We didn't go out to buy formula or diapers. We didn't collect clothes or bedding from friends. We left the "children's study" exactly as it was.

Finally, we got word that we would be able to take custody of the baby at 4:40 P.M., Wednesday, in the lawyer's office. The Bergers would pick up the child at the hospital and deliver him to us. We would be alone in their office, waiting for them, and would have no way of knowing what might be happening there. If there were going to be a change of mind, this was one of the most likely times for it to happen. The girl had signed a preliminary voluntary-relinquishment form a couple of days earlier, but we had scarcely noted the event. The signature on that paper meant nothing. The baby was everything.

In one of her recent calls, Celeste had asked me what the name of the baby would be. I said we did not want to give him one until after we had taken custody. The legal documents required that he have a name, Celeste insisted. When we picked him up, she would need that information. So Susan and I had to discuss names. There was no question that my children's play, *In the Nick of Time,* and the name of the agency in Colombia, La Casita de Nicolás, contributed to our choice. We looked Nicholas up in the dictionary of names we had carried around for years. It meant "Victorious Army." I expected Susan, with her pacifist leanings, to reject the name simply on the basis of the meaning. To my surprise, she did not. That, she said, was exactly what we needed, a survivor—not a Thomson, who had died at three days, nor a Jonathan, whose name meant "God Given." What God gives, God can take away. Victorious Army was much better. Even so, we thought and spoke of him still as "the baby"—as if there were a name in our hands and a baby in someone else's. Until he came where the name was, it did not count. It was, like the exchange taking place across town, an abstraction. There was no Nicholas until we held him in our arms. But then he would be Nicholas with a vengeance.

We arrived downtown forty minutes early. Wanamaker's was just a block away. Susan insisted we stop there. She was out of panty hose. We would pretend nothing out of the ordinary was going to happen.

Even so, it was only 4:00 P.M. when we arrived at the lawyer's office. The secretary let us in. She soon left for the day, and we waited alone. We heard the sounds of other offices emptying, of people going home. The building became quiet in the way only an empty skyscraper could be quiet. Nat Berger specialized in labor-arbitration law. I leafed through his textbook on the subject. He also had a large collection of frogs: ceramic frogs, stuffed frogs, frogs in human garb, frogs asleep, frogs hung over, frogs as footstools, frog families. The frogs stared at us from under heavy lids. I remembered we had gone to the restaurant Frog the day we did not take custody of Jonathan. That was almost two and a half years ago. I saw the half bath stuffed to the ceiling with baby furniture. We waited.

As the time passed—it was now 5:45—it became clear that something had gone wrong. At the latest, Celeste had expected to be back in the office by 5:30. I tried not to think about what might have delayed the release. Neither of us spoke of it. Susan was panicking. She suggested it might help to play a game. What about Animal, Vegetable, Mineral? I couldn't remember one time in the eight years I'd known her that she'd ever wanted to play a game. I was surprised she even knew one, although not that she didn't get the name quite right.

We played the game aimlessly. Speaking, without hearing. Responding, without thinking. There was the noise of the elevator and someone walking in the hall. We stopped, paralyzed. Someone put something down. There was no sound of a baby. We heard a broom. It must be a janitor.

We gave up the game. It wasn't working. 6:30 came. We waited in silence. What would life be like if someone came through the door without a baby? How could we stay in that room much longer? There was no one we could call. We were not even supposed to know in what hospital the baby had been born. We knew, but the knowledge was as useless as the frogs that kept silent vigil with us.

Again there was the sound of the elevator and someone getting off. We stared silently at the door that was opening. Celeste walked in. She carried the yellow blanket we had supplied. In it was Nicholas.

Susan Celeste handed me the bundle. We looked in. Nicholas had a pointed head. He had a lot of hair. His eyes were closed. One hand, with long, graceful fingers, was curled over the edge of the blanket. The magnitude of his being there, the weight of that bundle, inspired silence. I stood there awkwardly. I was aware of Ken as much as of the baby. He stood beside me just as awkward, just as quiet. Wasn't he a doll? said Celeste matter-of-factly.

The hospital, she told us, had sent some supplies and a few baby-care samples. She unpacked the diaper bag, pointing out the six four-ounce disposable bottles of formula, which should at least get us through the night. A stuffed elephant fell out of the bag. Celeste hurriedly thrust it into a desk drawer. We obviously were not supposed to see that. She did not, however, lose a beat. The delay, she went on, had been caused by the hospital, which had not circumcised the baby until that day, presumably because of the jaundice. The hospital wanted to keep him until the doctor was sure he was urinating properly. There were a few odds and ends of paperwork that had to be completed, she continued. She needed our check for the rest of the hospital fees. There might be a few more medical expenses yet to come. If so, she would send us the bills. She also needed at the moment our signatures on several papers. Ken gave her our check and signed his name several times as Celeste directed him. I reluctantly handed him Nicholas, and I, too, signed my name. I trusted him to know what the papers were. Now, what was the baby's name? asked Celeste. Nicholas Viguers Arnold, said Ken.

Nicholas seemed warm. He didn't need quite so many clothes, I stated—tentatively. Celeste led me into the next room where there was a large, empty desk, and while I stood by, she unwrapped him and took off a couple of layers of clothing. Nat arrived from parking his car, and Ken left to bring ours around to the front of the building. I heard him run down the hall to the elevator. Ten minutes later, I left the office with Nicholas.

It was raining. Holding Nicholas tightly against me, I dashed out of the building lobby and ducked into the car. Ken gunned the engine and the car sped off. He felt, he said, like a bank robber after the biggest heist of his career. He turned the car back onto Broad Street. The bright oval of the tower clock on City Hall showed seven o'clock.

"Why doesn't he make any sounds?" I asked. "Maybe he's just sleepy," suggested Ken. I didn't think so; his eyes kept opening. Halfway home, Nicholas made his first cry. It sounded like a meow. "What kind of voice is that!" said Ken, obviously delighted. We laughed together. It occurred to me that Ken was driving very fast. I remembered it was dangerous to carry a baby in a car. Nicholas should be in his own seat. Here we'd had him for twenty minutes and we were already doing something wrong. It felt good to be typical parents.

When we got home, Ken leapt out of the car and unlocked the front door so I could run in. He wanted his turn to hold his son. Our families would be waiting nervously far away in Massachusetts and Virginia. We phoned and told them our news. Now for a couple of friends in Philadelphia. I called Peshe and Linda with the brief message, "He's here." Fifteen minutes later, Linda arrived, and then Peshe and Peter, laden with a bassinet, bags full of baby linen and clothes, and champagne. We sat in the kitchen and drank champagne. Nicholas lay first in Ken's arms and then in mine, looking around sleepily, occasionally grunting, gurgling, or sneezing. Ken took photographs. I realized Nicholas had not been changed. We had not unclothed him enough to see his feet. I felt ridiculously timid. Ken did too. Linda said she would help. We unwrapped him. His umbilicus was a raw stump, his newly circumcised penis looked strange, but he had two arms, two legs, ten perfect fingers, ten perfect toes. We marveled. I changed him. He peered cautiously from between narrowly parted eyelids. I put a bottle in his mouth. He sucked it.

Linda asked if we'd like her to go to a store to buy some bottles, formula, and diapers. I recalled the supplies we'd bought for Jonathan. Ken had stuck them into the top of a third-floor closet. I'd been aware they were there but had never looked at them carefully. Now I gave Nicholas back to Ken, ran upstairs, and brought the supplies down. The expiration date on the formula had passed, but the bottles and diapers were still usable—as was the edition of Dr. Spock we'd purchased just after Jonathan's birth.

After our friends left, Ken dug the portacrib out of the third-floor storage closet. He put it at the foot of our bed, and we laid Nicholas in it. The "children's study" for the night would remain unchanged. By the time we went to bed, it was already past midnight. Nicholas woke hourly throughout the night. On the half hour we checked for breathing and other vital signs. By morning the day's excitement and the lack of sleep left us both haggard. Driven by some sort of mad compulsion, Ken went off to work. I changed Nicholas, fed him part of a bottle, and dozed off. An hour later Ken was back. After a half hour at the office, he said, people had begun to notice that they had to repeat everything before he understood what they were saying, and his boss, David, ordered him to go home.

The first week was filled with celebration and activity fueled by nervous energy. We fixed up the nursery. Friends dropped off more baby furniture and clothes. Ken's sister Karen called and asked how soon was not too soon to come. She drove up from Virginia with their father for the day, bringing a crib, high chair, car seat, and a box of cloth diapers and linen, all once used by her own children. Several times during the afternoon, I saw Ken's unabashed pride as he watched his father cradle Nicholas and make faces at him.

The dean of my department, Pat Cruser, had arranged to fix dinner for us on Saturday night. We were not to worry about anything. At 6:30, to our surprise, thirty-five people showed up bringing food and gifts. Nicholas lay peacefully in a carriage and slept. The group left us with an absolutely clean kitchen, taking with them several large plastic bags filled with trash. Ken and I had planned a dinner party for the next day long before we knew when or if Nicholas might come along. We decided to make the meal simple but to go ahead with it. One of the guests was a friend of Ken's, a priest. He blessed Nicholas and said he would read Psalm 113, appointed by the church calendar for that Sunday's service. As usual, I was ill at ease with the introduction of the religious into the secular. But when I heard the psalm, its timing in the church calendar seemed providential. It concludes: "He makes the mother of a childless house / To be the joyful mother of children."

The next day my semester of teaching was beginning. Ken cleaned up after our guests that Sunday night, and I worked at my typewriter trying to finish up my course descriptions and requirements. I had the illusion of constructing fictive courses for someone else to figure out and execute: it was impossible to believe I'd be teaching in a few days.

Dean Cruser covered the first meeting of my classes, but later in the week I returned for the next ones. Ken had worked out, informally, an arrangement with David whereby he stayed at home four half days a week for the first month, taking care of Nicholas while I was teaching. Since Nicholas would sleep, we hoped, much of those first weeks, it would be possible for Ken to do some work at home. I would be home the rest of the time and was, like Ken, depending on Nicholas to sleep so I'd have time to do my school work.

Nicholas was, in fact, settling in quite quickly. When awake, he was always on the move. He would work his way to the edge of a bed within minutes. He loved to hang upside down. Bat-baby, we called him. He drank well. He began to chortle. And if we planned it right, he began waking only once a night. We took turns getting up with him when he woke during the nights and alternated feedings when we could during the day. When we were together, we fought over who would hold him; I was convinced he realized this and was amused by it. We had fallen in love with him—in the same powerful, physical way that one falls in love as an adult with another adult. I had expected that. But Ken seemed genuinely amazed. The only thing for which I was not prepared was how much I missed my parents. I sang Nicholas the lullabies of my childhood and wept that my mother and father would not know this miracle, my son.

Ken could not continue too long staying home four half days, even with a cooperative Nicholas. After a month we would begin a new arrangement. I set up a nursery in my office and hired a student to sit for Nicholas during my afternoon class hours. Dinnie, the young woman we'd hired when we thought we were adopting Jonathan, would take care of Nicholas at home the two mornings I taught. Those days, Ken would go to work a little late. It all sounded possible.

We were anxious about the scheduling for only one reason. As in all private adoptions, the city would send out a social worker to begin evaluating our suitability as parents. There would be two visits. The Department of Social Welfare would arrange the first to take place before the Voluntary Relinquishment. We both agonized about that Voluntary Relinquishment. It would be then that the biological mother and grandmother would be asked a second time if they had any doubts about giving up parental rights. The birth mother could change her mind with no questions asked anytime up to and including the day of the hearing. Although the hearing could occur after thirty days, the Philadelphia court system being what it was, some hearings were delayed for sixty days or even longer. How quickly our case went through the system depended a lot on our social worker. We were eager to get to know her. We were also uneasy about the interview. What would she be looking for? Would the fact that both of us had continued working be a problem? We hoped the fact that one of us was with Nicholas at all times for the first month would help convince a potentially skeptical social worker that we could manage two careers and a child simultaneously. After the Voluntary Relinquishment hearing, there was to be a surprise visit from the social worker, to take place before the Final Adoption Decree. What if the dishes weren't done? What if the social worker called up and we were out? We could, Ken suggested, put an answering machine on our telephone so that the social worker would have no way of knowing whether or not we were at home. Linda told me we were being unbelievably paranoid. For one thing, babies were not expected to be kept in the house every day for months.

There was, however, another reason for thinking about an answering machine. We wanted to know what people were trying to reach us, if possible, before they succeeded. We would leave the country, we decided, if it looked like a move to regain custody of Nicholas was in the offing. We felt the same way about that, though, I was quite aware, we never discussed anything more definite. Where would we go? How could we begin over, totally new, in another country, cut off from friends and family? I couldn't let myself think about it. But still, the assumption that we would leave was the only thought that was emotionally possible. One of my colleagues told me she had been discussing us with a friend who was a family therapist. He had commented how difficult it must be; adoptive parents must deal with the anxiety of the wait, he had said, by postponing bonding. I relayed the conversation to Ken. We laughed until we cried.

The Kuriloffs had a friend who was a social worker in the Department of Public Welfare. Perhaps she could give us some information, from the inside, on what to expect. Ken called and explained our worries. She was convinced that our case would be one a city social worker, beset by difficult and painful cases, would in fact relish.

Several times a week visitors would come by to see Nicholas. The women from my group. Friends from Ken's office. Mary Pearson, our next-door neighbor, who made us promise we would call if she could be of any help. She had just retired, after forty years of working—most recently as a precision grinder in a ball-bearing factory. She had free time. That same day the Zeitlins, my first parents-in-law, with whom I stayed in contact after my divorce, stopped by. Abe was a violinist and Reba a pianist. One of the few details Ken and I learned about Nicholas's biological relatives was that the aunt in Boston was a professional violinist. Maybe Nicholas would be musical. We could at least hope. Abe agreed that Nicholas's fingers seemed unusually long. That, he commented, could be even more useful for the piano than the violin.

Since I'd begun my medication, I decided to go through the cycle as usual on my thermometer, Clomid, progesterone regimen. In spite of our exhaustion, Ken and I made love as scheduled by my chart. At the end of the first week of February, I went in for my monthly blood test and gynecological exam. It was Dr. Boger who took my blood this time. He was incredulous that I'd actually been trying to get pregnant this month. I enjoyed his amazement and, for once, didn't care that the blood test would be negative. Dan Meyer greeted me warmly. How was Nicholas? He wanted to meet him—or at least see pictures. I promised I'd bring him to my next appointment. I was a success.

That next week, the social worker at the Children's Aid Society of Philadelphia called. Were we interested, she asked, in proceeding further with an adoption through that agency? She sounded genuinely pleased when I told her we actually had a baby. Was I relieved we wouldn't be adopting a black-white, a biracial, baby? I wasn't sure. I was tired of self-examination. I shelved the question. I was too much in love with Nicholas—and too anxious that we would have to fight for him.

The city social worker phoned and arranged for a visit

for February 21. The previous Thursday, Debby and her family drove down from Massachusetts for a several-day visit. They had loaded their car with things David had outgrown. Debby had been saving them for her second child. She, too, had been wanting to get pregnant, but now after years of trying she and Dennis had pretty much given up, and they wanted Nicholas to have the clothes and toys. Debby brought my parents closer. Her son, also, had never known them. She had become pregnant with David just after their deaths. When she came home with him from the hospital, I flew up to Massachusetts to be with her. I was needed and wanted, but I knew I could not make up for the absence of my parents. Debby understood what I was feeling now.

We talked about how much our parents would have enjoyed Nicholas's being Chinese. Both my mother and father had taught in China in the thirties and had in fact met and married there. We three daughters actually had a film of their wedding—my mother as she was carried in a Chinese chair, draped with richly embroidered hangings, and my father, looking a little dazed, standing in a garden, next to a dragon gate. My father had studied Chinese and written several articles about China—even a book, which had the bad luck of being printed at the very moment the printing plant was bombed by the Japanese. One thing I had taken with me after my parents died was my mother's carved, lacquered Chinese hope chest. I reminded Debby that in it was a blue, brocaded formal Chinese robe, which had belonged to our father. When Nicholas grew up, that robe would be his—a gift from his grandfather.

The social worker came for her first visit. It was immediately obvious that her study would not be the kind of in-depth evaluation that we'd experienced in our previous homestudies. We were assumed to be acceptable parents. She just needed a lot of information—mostly about what we owned and more generally our financial profile. She asked us how many rooms were in the house, but it was clear that she didn't feel the need to look through them. Nicholas woke up from his nap, and I brought him down so she could meet him. We had questions for her too; the most important was about the Voluntary Relinquishment hearing. She didn't think we should worry about it. As far as she understood, the case looked secure. Ken asked when the hearing would be. We were just a little too late for the next session of hearings, so we would have to wait for the one afterward. When would that be? I asked. It would be another couple of months. In the past it wouldn't have been that long, but the judge had recently decided to hear Voluntary Relinquishments every sixty rather than every thirty days. It took a moment for the information to sink in. I broke into tears. Ken in fury attacked the cruelty of making us wait in limbo sixty more days. Was this supposed to be an endurance test?

The social worker did not seem prepared for such an emotional reaction. We pleaded with her to pressure the judge at family court to put us on the docket for March 12. She promised she would try. Two long days later, she called to tell us she had succeeded.

Three days before the social worker's visit, Ken had returned to his office full-time and I had begun taking Nicholas to work. The previous week I'd brought in baby supplies: a bassinet, sheets, blankets, diapers, formula, bottles, nipples, a few crib toys, and a mobile. I had asked my students if any wanted a baby-sitting job and had had several volunteers. I chose one young woman who had the most flexible schedule and seemed the most enthusiastic. I again cleared with Dean Cruser my having Nicholas at school. Everything was ready.

The first day worked out perfectly. My classroom was only a few doors away from my office, so I could easily be reached if necessary. But Nicholas, the sitter told me, slept, took a bottle, chortled for a while, and fell asleep again. Still, I couldn't help feeling a little guilty. I claimed that bringing him to school was the only way we could solve a complex child-care problem, but we hadn't considered alternatives simply because I wanted Nicholas there. More than that, I delighted in his being there. I asked several of my colleagues if he was a distraction. They seemed to like my bringing him in. I was lucky. After my classes and conferences, I changed Nicholas and packed him into the baby carrier. A woman in the elevator exclaimed how tiny he was. He was only five weeks old, I told her. The woman complimented me on how quickly I'd regained my figure; I must have been exercising all along. "I never stopped," I said, privately enjoying the joke.

The Voluntary Relinquishment hearing fell on a Thursday. We debated staying home from work, but sitting there waiting all day would be intolerable. It was best to pretend it was like every other day. The meeting that was to decide our fate, and Nicholas's, was across the city, involving people we did not know and who did not know us. Adding to our anxiety, the birth mother and grandmother were now living in Boston. What if they ran into problems traveling and didn't get to Philadelphia in time? That wouldn't necessarily mean they wanted Nicholas back, but it *would* mean an unbearable extension. We would find out what had happened only when the hearing was over. The city social worker suggested we call her at about 2:00 P.M. It was not clear to us just how we would be informed if the birth mother changed her mind and decided to take custody. We felt too threatened to ask. We prepared to go to work as usual in the morning, leaving Nicholas with Dinnie. I would be home by about noon. We left instructions that under no circumstances was Dinnie to tell anyone where Nicholas was, that she was to say he was with us and she did not know where we were. What we planned to do, we had no idea. Until I left work, Ken or I called home hourly, just in case.

At exactly 2:00 P.M. I phoned the social worker. She did not have any information. The judge had adjourned for an unusually long lunch. The hearings were not over yet. About an hour later, the social worker called. All was well. The biological mother had formally relinquished custody of the child. We had nothing more to worry about. I phoned Ken with the news. Immediately after hanging up, the phone rang again. It was the Bergers, in the past so conservative, but now completely reassuring. It would be very difficult for the biological mother to regain custody after this, they told me.

Nicholas was in the middle of his afternoon nap. I went into his room—no more the "children's study"—picked him up, held him tightly, and wept. He was quite astonished—and not at all pleased to be awakened.

Ken had been scheduled for several months to deliver a paper that evening on sources for American playwriting, and I wanted to hear what he had to say. Dinnie came back to sit, and we left Nicholas with a confidence we had never felt before. An enormous burden had been lifted from our shoulders. When we got home, I dug out of the third-floor closet a nursery-rhyme book I had bought three years before for Jonathan. Ken inscribed it "To Nicholas Viguers Arnold, on the third important day of his life. Love from Mama and Papa, March 12, 1981."

The first, of course, was his birth. The second was the day he came to us. The fourth would be the day of the Final Adoption Decree. We might have to wait as long as ten months for that hearing. Emotionally, we chose to accept the lawyer's assurance that everything was now all right. Even if the biological mother changed her mind, we would now have a real legal basis on which to claim Nicholas. We wouldn't fail.

The next visit of the social worker wasn't a surprise. She called ahead of time to be sure we'd be there. It didn't make sense to make a trip for nothing. She exclaimed at how Nicholas had changed. Everything was going smoothly, she told us.

Nicholas continued to go to my office two days a week. He became a kind of mascot for the department. One particularly large chair in Dean Cruser's office provided a perfect place for him to sleep on those occasions when I had to attend a meeting and a student wasn't available to sit. The secretaries kept an eye on him there. For the most part, I scheduled student conferences for the two mornings when Nicholas would not be with me. Gradually I found, however, that his presence was a benefit to some conferences, especially those with problems. Students seemed less inclined to see me antagonistically if a baby was crying or sleeping in the corner of the office, or if they found themselves holding him while I prepared a bottle or left for a moment to wet a cloth in the ladies' room. As the semester went on, I began to take him to more and more faculty and committee meetings. He would lie in my lap, drinking his bottle and looking around intently. Several times his resonating burps were declared the most intelligent comments of the afternoon. As my committee assignments proliferated, I felt less guilty about bringing him. His portability was the only thing that made it possible for me to meet extra responsibilities.

One day I was standing outside Anderson Hall, talking to Lily. Nicholas was in a stroller. Lily's eight-year-old, half-Chinese son was hopping from foot to foot impatiently, though somewhat intrigued, in spite of himself, by Nicholas. A student of Lily's came by and exclaimed what a beautiful baby Lily had. Lily's laughter bubbled over. She wished she could take credit, she responded, but actually he wasn't hers. The woman had assumed Daniel was mine and Nicholas was Lily's. Adopted children were not the only ones who didn't look like their parents.

Later in the spring, when extra meetings came at times that would be awkward for Nicholas, I took him next door to Mary Pearson's apartment. Mary insisted that we not pay her. After all, she said, she was his neighborhood grandmother.

On several occasions, Ken took Nicholas to his office, propping him up on the desk in his car seat or hanging him in a Jolly Jumper swing in the doorway. He was becoming very active; we thought he might be an early walker. Ken had walked at nine months. One evening when Ken brought Nicholas home, he had a wonderful story for me. He had been walking across campus with Nicholas in his back carrier on the way to pick up some lunch when he had run into a Chinese acquaintance, who was editing a book for him. Ray exclaimed that he hadn't realized Ken had a baby. Yes, said Ken proudly, and he introduced Nicholas. Ray glanced at him periodically as he and Ken talked about the book they were working on. "You know," Ray commented, as he was about to go his own way, "your son's hair is so straight and black, it could almost be Chinese."

 Ruth

Ken One day when Nicholas was four months old, I opened a letter from La Casita, expecting a new form or worse. A dark, poorly focused Polaroid photograph of a small, solemn baby on a nun's lap fell out. It was the way the agency informed couples that a baby was waiting for them. Susan had claimed she didn't expect it to happen. I hadn't shared that pessimism, but I had certainly assumed a much longer wait. I scanned the enclosed letter, which, as usual, was in Spanish. I made out that the baby was a girl, three months old, named Elena Lucia Román and was, according to the letter, *"muy simpática."* I had a daughter! The next moment I also realized that we would have twins.

Though it was both after the end of the spring semester and six o'clock in the evening, Susan was still at work, chairing a search committee. When I called the college, I was told that she was in a meeting in the president's conference room and could not be disturbed. Fortunately, I recognized the voice of a friend at the other end

151

of the line. I persuaded her that news of the arrival of her baby was sufficient cause to call a mother out of a meeting.

That night we wired a reply to Colombia: WE ARE EXCITED ABOUT ELENA AND CANNOT WAIT TO BRING HER HOME. WE WILL NAME HER RUTH VIGUERS ARNOLD.

What about Nicholas? Would his presence jeopardize our adopting Ruth? Pat Smith told us there would probably be about a two-month wait before we'd be able to go and pick her up. That would come just about the time we were hoping Nicholas would have his final adoption hearing—a date for which we obviously had to be in Philadelphia. The first step, we decided, was to complete the final paperwork for Ruth. When we knew definitely about Nicholas's hearing date, we would write La Casita about Nicholas and the date of his hearing. Susan thought it might help to talk in the letter about being a twin herself. We could make a case for how good it would be for the two babies to grow up together. It all sounded logical. But was honesty going to hurt us? Alternatively, we could omit mentioning Nicholas. We could say we couldn't come to Colombia at the time of his hearing because of something about my job. But that sounded weak, and we didn't want to lie. Our two children were vying for attention at the same time. Even before we actually had the second. We were being prepared for the future.

We again found ourselves in the bureaucratic web of foreign adoption. We had to contact the social worker who had done our homestudy and get permission to take an extra copy of the study to Colombia. Pat Smith warned Susan that we should have a couple of copies of all our papers with us in case there were some kind of foul-up. I thought Susan was being paranoid about the possibility of problems until she told me what had happened to Pat with her first baby. When she and her husband arrived in Bogotá, they found that the U.S. Embassy would not provide a visa for their son because he did not have a health certificate from Medellín. Pat was directed to return her baby to Medellín for six weeks to get the document. The embassy doctor finally agreed to see the child and provide the necessary papers. Then they discovered the visa approval had not arrived from Philadelphia. The embassy tried to call Immigration in Philadelphia, but operators were unable to get through. That meant staying in Bogotá one more day. To make matters worse, Pat's visa was due to expire in twenty-four hours. That next day one operator came in early to place the call for them and approval was given, though there was some complication because the person who had reviewed the visa application in Philadelphia five weeks before was no longer working there. Finally, they were ready to go home. The embassy called ahead to hold the plane, which was due to take off in one hour. When they arrived, they found the plane had left. No other flights were scheduled that day for Philadelphia or Miami. As a last resort they approached Braniff Airways about a flight to New York. After a rapid exchange in Spanish between two clerks, they were told that the flight had left twenty minutes before but had mechanical problems and was returning. They could board that flight. Pat's experience was characteristic of those of others in that somehow, in spite of unforeseen crises, everything worked out. Nonetheless, her story was unsettling. We were determined to prepare for as many problems as possible.

We made a list and divided up the calls and jobs. Susan was basically responsible for Harrisburg and getting Pennsylvania approval. I took responsibility for dealing

with Immigration. Immigration would okay a visa petition only after they received notification that the state
would accept the adoption. Susan took the train to Harrisburg, to the Bureau of Child Welfare, armed with the
homestudy, Ruth's abandonment decree, birth certificate, and our divorce and marriage certificates. All went
well. Only one document was missing: Ruth's health certificate. Susan promised to send it as soon as we received
it. Just as Pat Smith had directed her.

I set up an appointment with Immigration later that
week. I asked our friend Tom Goodman, who was fluent
in Spanish, to translate the abandonment decree and
Ruth's birth certificate. Both the originals and translations
would be necessary for U.S. Immigration. Our fingerprint
files were still valid. So that major project was done. I was
directed to come with my wife to the infamous Immigration room #1321 in the Federal Court Building. There
we joined rows and rows of non-Americans waiting endlessly to be processed. I felt like an alien. I wondered how
long we would have to wait. I needed to get back to the
office before the afternoon. We took a number and sat
down. Others, it was clear, had been there for a long time.
Every few minutes a clerk called a number and one of the
otherwise passive petitioners would go to one of the windows that lined one side of the room. I was tempted to ask
for a quarter pound of ham. After only a short while,
however, a man appeared and called my name, and we
were led into the offices behind the windows. Obviously,
Susan remarked, Americans were presumed to have less
time to waste than "foreigners."

I agreed to be the formal petitioner. I presented my
birth certificate, marriage certificate, our bank statements, income-tax forms, homestudy, and Ruth's aban-

donment decree and birth certificate (with translations).
I explained that we did not have an adoption decree,
because we would be adopting the baby in this country
afterward. It was not true. In Harrisburg, Susan had said
we would be adopting in Colombia. Harrisburg and Immigration had different rules. Harrisburg would not easily
approve the adoption unless they were told it would take
place in Colombia. If we did not have a final decree in
hand, Immigration would not easily accept the petition
for a visa unless there were to be adoption proceedings in
the States. We were taking advantage of a loophole to
simplify Ruth's adoption. If the discrepancy in our claims
were noted, the best procedure would be to stall for time
until the final decree arrived from Colombia. That would
satisfy everyone. The worst that could happen was that
we would be forced to start adoption proceedings in the
States while waiting for the decree from Colombia. That
would mean another homestudy, more paperwork,
money, time, but no one would take our baby away. Still,
I was uneasy lying just when I wanted to be the epitome
of a responsible citizen-parent. Immigration agreed to
cable the approval for the petition of Ruth's visa to the
American Consulate in Bogotá. Everything looked fine.
Susan and I breathed a sigh of relief and went out for a
brief lunch to celebrate.

There were a few more necessary preparations. We
needed passports, and we had to send to Bogotá a "request for adoption" form. That had to be notarized and
stamped at the Colombian Consulate. Susan had previously dealt with the consulate, but this time it was necessary that we both go. I looked forward to it. My first official
introduction to a country I'd been so unaware of and that
now had become so important. The consulate was located

in a small two-room office in Philadelphia. The first thing
I noticed was a large topographical map of Colombia on
the wall. I was startled at the mountainous center where
the major cities were. So that was Bogotá. I could see no
reason to put a city there, high on a plateau, far from
rivers and the coast. I looked curiously at the officials and
the people waiting in the room. I liked the looks of them.
I was suddenly eager to be among those mountains and
more of Ruth's people.

The next week we learned that Nicholas's final adoption hearing was scheduled for July 24. Susan drafted a
letter to La Casita, telling the people there about him.
Carmela and John were leaving shortly for Colombia and
offered to take the letter with them. They were confident
La Casita would not be disturbed to hear about Nicholas.

It was a busy period for other reasons as well. A political crisis at Susan's college was taking up much of her
time. She was also determined to get the garden in order,
as well as do some jobs around the house, in preparation
for Ruth's arrival. She attacked the plastering with an
amateur's enthusiasm and skill. I was busy at the office,
trying to tie things up. We planned to leave for our usual
two-week Rhode Island vacation at the beginning of July.

On top of everything else, at a party a week before the
arrival of Ruth's letter, I had gotten into a slightly
drunken discussion with one of Susan's officemates. Besides being a philosopher, he was a carpenter, and we
discussed his turning part of our shabby back screened
porch into a room off the kitchen. If we were ever to do
such a project, now was the time. We needed the room,
and once the second baby arrived, the disruption would
be difficult. So the house was filled with plaster dust and
the din of construction.

Also, there was the matter of the cottage Susan's aunt owned in Rhode Island. Aunt Doris, now eighty-three, had finally decided that it would be to everyone's benefit if she sold it to the three sisters rather than will it to them. I worried about a family enterprise. And how were we going to handle three major expenses—the porch, the cottage, and, most important, the trip to Colombia? In the end, we decided we would manage it all. The money for the trip would come from the last of Susan's inheritance, a link with her parents that she liked. For the other projects we would take a loan.

Finally, a student named Celia who worked at my office was unexpectedly stranded without an apartment for the summer. I wanted to offer her a place to stay. I anticipated Susan's violent no. Didn't we have enough going on in our lives without adding another complication? But she finally agreed, so long as Celia would be gone by the time we came back with Ruth.

In the midst of all this, Nicholas chortled away. He grew his first tooth and began to crawl, or rather belly flop. He was both mobile and good-natured, carted back and forth to Susan's office, where she still maintained a nursery for him, back and forth to Mary's apartment next door, where he still had his portacrib.

We went to Rhode Island for two weeks, then up to Vermont for a weekend to visit Polly and Ken. We had cabled La Casita our itinerary and how to reach us at all times. While in Vermont, we received a call from Celia. A letter had arrived from Colombia. She didn't know Spanish, but with the help of a friend of Polly's in Vermont who did, we deduced that the news of Nicholas had not disturbed anyone. We were to come down to Colombia on August 8.

Susan brought Ruth's picture with us on our vacation. We couldn't leave our daughter at home. We studied it. What was she like? There was possibly a slight Oriental cast to her eyes. Several people said that from the photograph she looked a little like Nicholas. We constructed a personality from the picture. She was a determined little girl who would challenge her brother.

Susan kept musing about what she called fate. We had been given a Chinese son, and here she was with parents who had lived in China—a father who, especially, had been fascinated by that country. And now we were to have a daughter of Spanish heritage. Susan's mother had been fluent in Spanish. She had worked in Spain, establishing a children's library there, in the thirties. She had also been interested in Spanish dancing. Susan had a carafe that her mother had won dancing the flamenco in a Madrid café. We would give Ruth the castanets her grandmother had packed away in her Chinese hope chest. I liked our children having a China-loving grandfather and a Spain-loving grandmother.

On July 24 we went to family court with Nicholas. He sat on the conference table in the judge's chambers and smiled. The judge asked if anyone knew of any reason why we shouldn't adopt this child. "He's positively crowing," said one of the officials. A young man gave him a cup of water, which he promptly dumped on the table. Several people sprang to wipe it up. The judge asked us why we wanted to adopt him. Susan said, "Because we love him." That seemed a sufficient reason. So ruled.

We did not want to leave Nicholas just the next week. It was possible only because he was now legally, officially, ours. We had planned to take him up to Massachusetts to stay with Debby. But as the time drew near, we decided to simplify our trip by accepting the offer to take care of Nicholas made by one of Susan's colleagues at school, Nancy Davenport. She was the same one who back in May had put through to Susan my call about Ruth. The night before we were to leave, we took to Nancy's house the baby equipment, clothes, and pages of directions that Susan had been laboring over for days. Nancy insisted that she was going to love having a baby again, that Nicholas would be no problem.

The next morning we got up at five and took Nicholas to the Davenports. Nicholas probably wouldn't even miss us. We left him happily drinking a bottle of formula. Bill Davenport drove us to the airport. The first emotional trauma was over. We would not see Nicholas again for at least five days, perhaps two weeks.

We processed our tickets and checked our bags. A half hour later a voice on the public-address system announced that our Eastern Air Lines flight to Miami had been temporarily delayed. After a while we learned that a crack had been discovered in one of the engine mounts. Major repairs would be needed. The estimated delay: two hours. That meant that we might well miss our connecting flight to Colombia. No other airline was flying to Miami in time for us to make our plane. We would have to take our chances on this one. We waited for further news. The airline was flying in a part from New York. At a nearby welding shop, workmen were trying to repair the cracked mount. In my anger I was convinced that the airline had waited long enough to tell us the true nature of the problem and probable delay to ensure that we would all have to wait for the Eastern plane. Soon it became clear we would be "overnighted" in Miami. One more day without Nicholas, and without Ruth. I called

Colombia at Eastern's expense and left a message at La Casita that our arrival had been delayed until the same time the next day. After we waited nearly five hours, the plane was finally ready to leave.

In Miami, Eastern gave out vouchers for taxis, food, and lodging. We were directed to the Airliner Motel. There we were given two plastic bags each with a towel, washcloth, and a small bar of soap. The motel was right under the flight path for departing planes. Being "over-nighted" was not exactly gracious.

We deposited our things and went to supper in the dining room. We tried to make the best of our stay. Here we were, parents of two babies, out alone for the night. Other parents would envy us. The food, however, was wretched. And when I presented our voucher to the wait-ress, she told me we had already exceeded the amount. I had assumed we were being allotted fifteen dollars per person for dinner and breakfast; in fact that was supposed to cover both of us for two meals. Back in our room, I called Eastern's customer representative and told him how tacky I thought the airline was. Our ticket for the taxi ride to the motel hadn't even included a tip. The repre-sentative was well trained, polite, and unhelpful. He quoted regulations. I told him we'd missed picking up our baby daughter in Medellín and that Eastern owed us more than regulations. The man apologized. He sounded as though he were reading from a script. I couldn't touch him. I guessed that he was not permitted to hang up until I did, so I kept him on the phone for half an hour. Finally, as I knew I would, I hung up. With fury I told Susan that if we wrote a book about adoption, we should begin the story with this experience. It was symbolic, symptomatic of everything we'd gone through. I could tell Susan was uncomfortable with my outrage. At least she had sense enough not to urge me to calm down.

The next morning we at last boarded Avianca and left on time for Medellín. As we approached the city, I was mesmerized by the rugged terrain below. The earth was bunched almost as a series of waves crashing into the deep basin in which the city was sunk. The plane landed on a runway lined with people, entire families with picnic lunches who had come out to the airport to watch the planes. We fought our way through the crowd in the terminal. So many people, looking for what, for whom, speaking a language that sounded much more foreign than the Spanish on our Berlitz records. Pat Smith had said that each time she and her husband had come, their baby had been brought to the airport to meet them. Perhaps Ruth was here. We waited on the edge of the crowd. There were so many babies around. Almost every couple seemed to be carrying one. Susan was frantically anxious. Was that baby too old? That one too young? That one was obviously a boy, didn't I think? I left her, waiting, with the bags, and went to investigate the taxis. I returned in fifteen minutes. Still no Ruth. I was sure that our coming a day later had fouled up any possibility that she would be there. Susan agreed to leave after an hour. A painful hour, but no Ruth.

We finally got into a cab. I directed the driver to the country club, La Campestre, where we were to stay. It was my first effort in a long time at negotiating in Spanish. La Campestre was located just beyond the city limits. It had a large swimming pool outside the dining room, broad terraces leading to cool shaded walks under the palms, and brilliant flowering vines and trees everywhere. Towering over all were the distant mountains. The receptionist did not know English but knew who we were. We were outlanders, Americans who did not speak the language, oddities.

As soon as we dropped off our bags in our room, I tackled the Colombian phone system. I managed to get through to Evarista de Oliveira, the woman at La Casita with whom we'd principally communicated. She told me we were welcome to take a taxi to La Casita to see Ruth but that we wouldn't be able to pick her up until tomorrow. I reported the news to Susan, who was now in such a state of excitement that I felt calm by comparison. It was as though we were participating in a strange, dangerous game, as in a spy mystery. At each step we were given directions, which always involved some unseen complication, to the next step. But the total plan remained unknown.

The receptionist called a taxi. I gave the driver the address. After a few minutes he indicated he didn't understand it. I finally realized I had conflated an old address and a new one. La Casita had moved. I worked it out and settled back to notice the landmarks and learn as much as I could of the city. The taxi dropped us off in the dark street in front of a large stucco building fronted by an iron gate. We knocked on the door. It was answered by a nun, who, though she spoke no English, communicated that she knew who we were. She ushered us into a courtyard, told us to wait a moment, then slipped into a room off the courtyard. She returned with a small bundle and a bottle. With gesticulations, smiles, and a string of Spanish, she thrust the bundle into Susan's arms. It was dinnertime. Susan should feed the baby.

So this was Ruth. She was tiny and very pale. She had huge lemur eyes. Her little hands were very thin, but those and her face were all I could see. She was wrapped in several layers of clothing. Even her feet were swaddled in cloth. Her neck wobbled, and she obviously could not sit up. I thought of Nicholas, only a month older, who was so active that he seemed to bounce rather than fall and who was so delighted to be crawling. I missed him fiercely. I knew that Susan was not responding well, and I sensed she was struggling not to cry. She was trying to feed Ruth the bottle, but Ruth was not too interested. She was listless and, Susan whispered to me, very hot. She handed me the baby. I cradled her. How tiny and solemn she was. She was sweating. She held her hands in front of her folded together. Like a little nun. I handed her back to Susan. Several nuns had gathered. Two were feeding babies. A little boy with dark eyes and curly fair hair, about three years old, pulled on my leg. I bent down and tickled him, and the little boy doubled over in pleasure. The game became more elaborate. I swung the boy by his arms. Whenever I tried to stop, the child cried, *"Más, más"*—"More, I want more." A television in a corner of the courtyard was broadcasting a soap opera.

When Susan could no longer get Ruth to take any formula, the nun indicated we should put her to bed. We were led through the courtyard. We passed a play-pen in which a small grotesque figure lay on his back. He was the size of Nicholas, but he looked like an old man. The nun stopped, stroked his hair, spoke to him, and handed him a small truck that had fallen out of his hand. The figure smiled—a child's smile, not a baby's—and said something. We turned into a small room in which were four cribs, the room for newborns. In one crib was a miniature baby with blotchy red skin, a genuine newborn, probably a preemie. Susan asked about Ruth's diaper, and the nun communicated that she'd already been changed. When she took Ruth from Susan, she crooned to her in Spanish, and for the first time Ruth smiled. A brief smile, but a smile. "Did you see that?" I asked Susan with satisfaction. The nun placed Ruth on her back in the crib, covered her with a blanket, and stretched a mosquito net over the bed. She was immobilized, caged. She made no sound. We left her.

The cab ride back was quiet. I put my hand on Susan's, but I couldn't bring myself to talk. I was editing the previous scene. Ruth was weak, but not really that weak. She might have suffered some malnourishment, but it was nothing serious. There was that moment when she smiled. And after all, the situation was a strange one for her. Of course she was passive. Once we had her, that would change. The immediate business I had to focus on was getting back to the country club. I concentrated on recalling the streets, the intersections, giving halting directions in Spanish to the driver, who did not seem to know where to go. And yet we got there. Then the driver told me the fare. I quickly calculated it was equivalent to about fifty dollars. The trip downtown had cost five dollars. I was outraged. I gave the driver five dollars and, ignoring his protests, got out of the cab with Susan.

We went out onto the lawn around the swimming pool where people were sitting at tables talking and drinking. The regular dining rooms were closed. I ordered beer for both of us. We talked, tentatively, for the first time about Ruth. I continued to play down Ruth's condition. I could see Susan was upset. Yet I could think of nothing to do or say. I commented on the Latin form of drinking. A glass filled with rum or some other liquor accompanied by bottles of Coke. I was reminded of an occasion during my visit eight years before to Nicaragua when I had drunk too much home brew, chased with Coke, and had spent the evening throwing up into the lake.

Susan   That night I dreamed I gave birth to a baby who was, when I looked closely, a wizened old woman the size of an infant. I looked even closer and realized it was my mother, just before she died. When I woke, the dream seemed more real than the strange, chilly room, the unfamiliar sounds of water running in the room next door, and the clatter of a maid's cart in the hall outside.

I knew what I was going to wear. I had planned it for weeks. I had gone shopping and bought a thin, pale violet cotton blouse with a lace-edged collar. Luxuriating in a wave of sentimentality, I had thought, that's it, that's what I'll be wearing when I am given my daughter. When we had gone to pick up Nicholas in the lawyer's office, I'd superstitiously dressed myself with calculated unconcern as though I were going nowhere important at all. I had tried not to believe in his existence ahead of time. The situation now was different. I had no doubt: I had a daughter. But the knowledge carried with it something akin to terror. I was on a treadmill, which I myself was powering but could not stop. How could that tiny, thin baby lying quietly in the crib at La Casita be my Ruth? It was impossible to think of her as five and a half months old; she looked like a newborn. I clung to the thought of Nicholas. How was he? Was he sleeping all right? How was he eating? What if he threw a fit at bath time? I should have stressed that he didn't have to have baths. Did he miss us?

After breakfast, Ken called another cab and we went back to La Casita. When Ken had talked to Evarista on the phone, she said she would meet us there, but when we arrived, we found she had already left. She would be back, we were told, in about an hour. We were ushered into a front room to wait for Ruth to be bathed and dressed for her new parents. In that room, the "office," were several of the women who ran the agency, all but one of whom spoke English. They were warm, but preoccupied. Two couples had just left the previous week with babies from La Casita, and there was another couple besides ourselves coming this week. There was a great deal to do. One woman asked if we would help the other couple, also Americans, get adjusted to the country club. I had a sense that while the nuns moved slowly and methodically caring for the children, the women who ran the place dashed in and out of the orphanage, managing with skill both busy outside lives and their activities at La Casita. They were volunteers—wealthy Colombian businessmen's wives who had chosen La Casita as their charity. They were elegant and visibly upper-class. One woman asked us how the weather was in the States. Because of the current heat wave she had recently changed her mind, she said, about accompanying her husband to New York, where he was at the moment. Later I heard her speak of a shopping trip to Paris. On the other hand, the women seemed deeply committed to the orphanage. I deduced from several comments that at least a few of the women not infrequently took a child home with them for a weekend, especially children who were older or more difficult to adopt. One was the strange little grotesque figure we had seen the evening before in the playpen. He was four years old, I found out, but had ceased growing as an infant; his visits to and tests in the hospital had not led to any improvement. Evarista's seven-year-old daughter was currently lugging him around and playing with him. Her affection for him was obvious, as was his pleasure. I was moved by the naturalness of it. But it was also frightening.

While we were waiting, I asked about Ruth. The women were enthusiastic. They assumed Ken's and my excitement, and I began to imagine that my response the night before had been premature; perhaps I had conjured up problems that did not exist. I asked about Ruth's health. She had been sick several times, we were told, but the doctor had seen her and she was fine. She had had her shots. She was a good baby. Evarista arrived—a tiny, elegant, bustling woman. She too spoke of our arrival and of "Elena" with warmth. One of the nuns in particular would be upset at "Elena's" leaving, Evarista said. "Elena" had been her favorite.

Finally, Ruth was brought in. She was clothed in an embroidered, slightly yellowed, starched white dress, with a petticoat, and tiny socks and cloth shoes. *"Muy linda, muy linda"*—"Very pretty"—the women cooed. She was handed to me. Ruth still looked like a little lemur. From the side, her eyes seemed sunken and her forehead protruded. From the front, she was all ears and eyes. Her shape was strange. The dress pulled tightly across her middle, but her shoulders and arms looked like little sticks. Her color was very pale, even pasty. This was the same baby I remembered from the night before: my daughter. Her large brown eyes stared at me intently, and she held on to one of my fingers with a viselike grip. She seemed frail, foreign, and intense. She had a rattle in her

chest—just a cold, Evarista reassured me. I felt I was acting in a play in a language I didn't know; it took all my
concentration to play my part.

We were taken through the orphanage, shown the
kitchen where a huge pot of soup was cooking (part of
Ruth's diet was a bottle of soup a day), the sleeping rooms,
and finally the open-air courtyard where we had first met
Ruth. There were many more children and babies than
were in evidence the night before. They came in almost
every color. Perhaps the most common, or, at least, the
most striking, were children with olive skin, huge brown
eyes, and loosely curling hair, fairer than their skin. The
majority of the children were toddlers, but there were a
few slightly older children and some infants. The babies
were all lying on their backs, either in infant seats or in
playpens, from which they could watch the activity of the
others. There were walkers and toys around, all of which
had seen better days but were still functioning. Although
there was a quality of everything being done en masse,
from eating to playing to sleeping, the children looked
healthy, even on the stocky side, and were engaged in
their world. It felt like an orphanage, but an impressive
one. Ruth was pale, quiet, and abnormal compared with
the babies and children filling the courtyard.

When we were ready to leave La Casita, "Ruth's nun"
patted her cheek and cried a little. She accompanied us
to the door. I carried my quiet, distant bundle. Evarista
planned to drive us home to the country club, but first, she
explained, she would take us to the grocery store where
we could buy what was necessary. We would need supplies for Ruth for one to two weeks. We'd brought a few
paper diapers, but mostly—to save on luggage—cloth
ones, and some clothes. As with the arrival of Nicholas,

friends had brought us bags and bags of clothes, many of which this time were particularly for girls. One afternoon, when I was deciding what to pack, I had tried a number of dresses on Nicholas to get a general sense of what would be the right size. Ruth would be a little smaller, we had thought, but in the same range. Nicholas had looked funny in the dresses; they didn't become him at all. Now I doubted whether the clothes we had brought would fit Ruth. But I couldn't bring myself to think of buying anything new. The most obvious need was for food and cooking supplies. The country club, Evarista told us, would supply us with hot plates.

Evarista took us to Exito, the local department store. It was like a gigantic Woolworth's, but included a complete food market. We stocked up on the only formula we could find, Nestogeno—the infamous formula distributed in third world countries by Nestlé—and jars of baby food, carefully choosing the foods Nicholas liked best and searching out the food to which sugar had not been added. The latter were by far the most expensive. We bought a pan for boiling water. We were worried about eating in the country-club restaurant, since our money was in short supply. But we knew we had to be somewhat careful about what and where we ate. Pat Smith had returned home from her second trip to Colombia with an amoeba that had put her in the hospital for several weeks and led to major surgery. Ken told Evarista we needed some food for ourselves. She guided us to the bread, the cheese, and finally to tables and tables of strange fruit. We passed the wine section. Ken chose one Chilean and two Argentinean wines. "We might as well take advantage of being in Colombia," he remarked. That sounded like Ken, and I was reassured. Ruth lay in my arms, so light when compared with Nicholas, sucking her thumb and watching—quietly. She did not appear to mind the stranger who was carrying her, but to me she seemed to have withdrawn even further into herself. I moved mechanically. I had to get through the present.

"One last thing to do," Evarista said; Ruth must have a picture taken for her visa. We left Ken at the check-out counter and went through the huge market and upstairs to a small room where a photographer had set up shop. Following Evarista's directions, I propped Ruth up with a pillow and held on to her from one side. Ruth's thumb was glued to her mouth; on Evarista's signal, I pulled it out for the picture. When I let go, without a murmur, Ruth snapped her thumb back into her mouth. I picked her up again. We rejoined Ken. Even he seemed in a daze. "We seem to be moving in," he said wryly as we gathered up our purchases.

Back at the country club, we found a crib had been set up in our room. Ruth was wet and smelled. She had to be changed. I remembered how timidly we had unwrapped Nicholas that first time in our kitchen, just six months before, with Linda, Peter, and Peshe sitting around the kitchen, toasting our new son. We had counted his toes. He was perfect. This time I wasn't timid; I was terrified. Ken and I unwrapped Ruth, carefully taking off La Casita's homecoming clothes. I had said I would wash and return them. Ruth had diarrhea. We gingerly unwound the complicated, three-layer cloth diaper wrapped around her and secured without pins or tape. She lay there, looking at us, her stomach a balloon that dwarfed her skinny arms and legs. I could not bear looking at her. One summer during my college years, I had worked as a nurse's aide at Children's Hospital in Boston and for a day had been put in charge of a tiny, severely retarded, malnourished baby, who had been left, forgotten for months, in some kind of institution before being "discovered" and brought to the hospital. It had been my job to tend her that day she was brought in, to take her for X rays and other tests. Everyone had assumed the baby would soon die, and I suddenly realized that I took for granted that she had. I remembered anesthetizing myself to that baby. I could never, however, forget the feel of her. Ken said he would change Ruth, and I felt a rush of remorse—what kind of mother was I—and gratitude. Ken was more sensitive to bad odors than I; I knew the diarrhea would bother him. He took a deep breath.

It was time to try to feed Ruth and put her down to sleep. She hadn't had a morning nap. I took comfort in trying to organize the room and our supplies. We would use cloth diapers and save the paper ones for traveling. Ken worked up his Spanish to ask for a hot plate. I heated up the soup the nuns had sent with Ruth, the Colombian equivalent, it seemed, of the standard hospital bundle sent home with Nicholas. Ruth would take little more than a sip. Ken claimed it didn't look appetizing anyway, that Nicholas wouldn't have liked it either. I decided we should try to make some formula. We were used to preparing formula for Nicholas, but this was different. It was clear that we shouldn't drink or give Ruth water from the tap. But was that water all right if we boiled it? One person I had asked had said yes, the second had said no. Evarista told us the country club supplied bottled water. Could we give that to Ruth? The first person I asked had said of course. The second, one of the women at La Casita, had recommended boiling even that. That settled it. We would boil the bottled water—but could we use the bottled water to wash Ruth's bottles, or did we need to wash them in boiled bottled water or even sterilize them? We hadn't sterilized Nicholas's bottles since he was a couple of weeks old, but in this case we should probably be on the safe side. Then there was the amount of powdered formula needed. Each bottle required approximately a quarter cup of formula. At that rate one container made at the most thirteen bottles (and the formula was much more expensive than any in the States). And, finally, the water I'd boiled proved to have cooled down too much to dissolve the powder. I reheated it. No wonder Nestogeno was such a problem. After all the work, Ruth was no more interested in the formula than she'd been in the soup.

I felt we should lay Ruth down on her stomach for her nap, though she was unused to that position. In the orphanage she had always been placed on her back, both asleep and awake, which maybe was sufficient reason in itself for her poor neck and arm muscles. She had had no opportunity to use them. Ken didn't think it wise to change the pattern so drastically. I rejected his point immediately. I knew he disliked my tone, but I couldn't bring myself to care. Perhaps, he continued, Ruth wouldn't understand that she had to keep her head turned and would smother. He should get credit for having some reason for his suggestions; I hardly had all the answers. I would sit by Ruth, I said shortly; we shouldn't leave her in a strange room by herself anyway. Fine, said Ken, he needed to check into getting more money changed—I obviously had things under control. When he left, it vaguely upset me that I wasn't angry with him or disgusted with myself. I felt too distant, too sunk into myself even to fight. Ruth lay in my lap, quietly, looking intently at me.

When I put her in the crib, Ruth didn't cry. She just lay there. There was no danger of her smothering. Her head remained as I had placed it. I dozed off. When I woke, I saw Ruth's eyes were open, fixed. Had she slept? Ken returned, and we decided to dress Ruth and take her with us down to one of the dining rooms, where we could have a bite to eat.

When we returned, we tried to feed her a jar of baby lamb and one of peaches. The food dribbled out of her mouth. Her tongue did not understand the spoon. She drank a little formula. The hours had dragged by. It was an appropriate time for her to go to bed. I dug out of her bag a silver and ivory teething ring that had been given to Nicholas. Ruth clasped it tightly. I put her in the crib—on her stomach. The loudest noise she had made was a low fuss. She still had not cried. The silence was weighted. Ken finally said he wanted to have a drink at the bar. I was tired and wanted to go to sleep. All I could think of was lying in bed, in the dark, curled up. I was awakened at one point in the night by the sound of Ken in the bathroom vomiting. Stomach problems on top of everything else. I assumed, fatalistically, that I, too, would come down with whatever he had.

That night my dreams were a confusion of nightmare and memory. I dreamed Ruth kept shrinking—growing smaller and smaller, until finally she was only a dot. Then she was gone. I was in my mother's hospital room. She was trying to brush her wild, curly gray hair, but she couldn't control her hand. I tried to brush it for her, but she screamed and pushed me away. She wasn't herself, the nurse said; the brain tumor and medication were seeing to that. I was a small child, and my mother was saying to me, "When you grow up, I hope you have a daughter as

special to you as you are to me." It was near the end. Her
hand lay on the hospital bed. She reached up for my hand,
but I was afraid. On the excuse of getting more water, I
left the room. I woke with a sense of battle fatigue and a
feeling of dread.

Ruth was in the same spot in which she had been put
the night before. That seemed unnatural. The teething
ring was still grasped firmly in her hand. We tried to
interpret that positively. It had to show something strong
about her. How many babies could hold on to a single
object all night?

Ken decided we should take some pictures. He put
Ruth on the bed in front of the glass doors of the balcony.
The mountains loomed in the background. He took two
shots of Ruth sitting propped up and several of her lying
on her stomach. I didn't want him to take the pictures, but
I couldn't think of any plausible argument against it. I
passively helped him arrange Ruth on the bed. What if
she were retarded? How could I go back to work in September? I couldn't imagine myself without a career—or,
at this point, with one. We had talked about putting the
children in a day-care center across the street from Ken's
office while I taught. In fact, we had even put down a
deposit. That was now obviously out of the question. And
what about Nicholas? He was well and strong. He might
not need me, but I surely needed him. What a strange way
to picture a six-and-a-half-month-old baby. I tried not to
think of any of it. As I'd done those months waiting for my
mother to die, I had to deal with things hour by hour, not
conceiving of the future.

At lunch we met the other American couple, Sarah
and Mat Taine. They had brought with them their eight-
year-old son, Andrew. For him the trip was obviously pure

adventure. He would no longer be an only child; he was getting a brother—and a trip to an exotic place. But his parents were just as obviously anxious. They, too, said they felt isolated, in spite of the warmth of the people at La Casita and La Campestre. It was clear we would be friends. Meeting them was like being thrown a life preserver. Sarah was a soul mate. The immediacy with which Ken, too, entered into the relationship surprised me. His Spanish was the best of the group, so he ordered everybody's lunch. Ken at his most charming.

The Taines had already picked up their son; he was a cherubic-looking, very active, bright little boy just under two years. Sarah looked at Ruth—so tiny, thin, and pale beside her chunky, healthy, demanding son—with something like pity. But for me it was a drink of reality; I wasn't crazy to be worried about Ruth. Sarah was also upbeat. She was sure, she said, that Ruth would start changing very quickly. And she had lovely eyes—even an adorable little cleft in her chin. The Taines hadn't found their introduction to their son easy either. He had been a favorite at La Casita and had spent considerable time outside the orphanage, staying with the volunteer women on weekends, and he wasn't at all sure he liked where he now found himself. The night before when they had put him down for bed, he had screamed for two hours. He talked quite well, but in Spanish: he was more engaged by the people around him at the country club who spoke Spanish than by his new family. I knew I would have found that hard.

The adoption procedure included seeing a doctor in Medellín to get a certificate of health. Pat Smith's story made it impossible for us to forget that step. The appointment was that afternoon. I awaited it apprehensively.

Maybe we could get some help with Ruth. To my relief
we arranged to go with the Taines, who had to get a
similar certificate for their son. We all sat in the waiting
room, watching a mother and her young son squabble
about something none of us, it turned out later, could
figure out. A nurse came out and called the Taines' name,
but Sarah motioned to us to go first. Gratefully and
quickly, I gathered up Ruth, and Ken led the way into the
next room. The doctor was sitting at his desk. On the wall
a framed diploma stated that he was a graduate of the
Mayo Clinic. That seemed auspicious to me. This would
be someone we could talk to, who would give us advice.
But when I started to undress Ruth, the doctor indicated
that that wouldn't be necessary. He poked her and stetho-
scoped her through her dress. "We're worried about her,"
I said. "She's so thin, and her stomach is bloated." "Let me
tell you," the doctor declared, "I have seen worse." Dead?
I felt like asking. "Listen to her chest," said Ken. "She is
sick." If we wanted medicine, the doctor said, he'd be glad
to give us a prescription, and he prescribed penicillin and
suggested we also buy Coricidin and something that
sounded like "sillygas," which he claimed would eat up
the gas that was bloating her stomach. He signed her
health certificate.

We returned to the waiting room, and Ken went out
to the pharmacy recommended by the doctor, while I
waited with Ruth for the Taines to finish with their appointment. Ken met us at the doctor's office about a half
hour later. He was empty-handed. The clerk in the pharmacy, he said, told him he did not have any penicillin or
"sillygas" but could give him the Coricidin. He described
the pharmacy as reminding him of a general store he
knew in southern Virginia, and he thought of buying over-

alls, crackers, grain for pigs. He chose not to fill the prescription. We would wait until we got home to follow our
own doctor's directions.

We found a cab to take us back to the country club but
decided to stop for supper before we got there. The most
convenient place was one that served the Colombian
equivalent of McDonald's hamburgers, *hamburguesas.*
To me they tasted like sawdust. Ruth was fussing; her cold
sounded worse. Sarah's sympathetic and understanding
presence was comforting only distantly. All I wanted was
to go back to our room. We walked the few blocks to the
country club along the smoke-choked highway. A constant line of cars passed us, and since there was no sidewalk, we walked single file. Ken remarked that he felt like
a refugee from an ecological disaster in a Grade B movie.
That image was exactly right.

The next morning, two days after Ruth's arrival, both
Ken and I woke up with colds. I had expected it; it was
almost a relief not to have to worry about catching one
anymore. We quickly finished the paper tissues supplied
by the club and started on the toilet paper. When we
finished that, Ken checked on the proper Spanish words,
tracked down one of the maids, and managed to communicate our need for more.

At least the official arrangements were going well. It
looked like we might get out of the country in less than
a week, something of a miracle. Evarista told us we did
not have to appear before a judge, that our application
was in order. We were scheduled to see the lawyer on
Wednesday and would be able to leave on Thursday for
Bogotá. That meant we could go home on Friday. Nicholas had never had a cold. I wondered if he could escape
this Colombian variety.

The lawyer's office was near La Casita. Evarista was scheduled to be at the orphanage. I decided we had to talk to her about Ruth's health. Ken felt that such questioning might breed misunderstanding about our feelings about La Casita. That, I said angrily, was just too bad. So Ken left Ruth and me at La Casita's front gate and went off to the lawyer's office. I stood there a moment, with Ruth in my arms, timid, after all, about asking questions. An outsider. The street was quiet. I knocked, and a moment later the door was opened. It was dark inside, after the bright afternoon light of the street.

Suddenly, Ruth began to cry—not a whimper but a strong, intense cry. It was a shock, a moment I will never forget. I was hearing for the first time my daughter's voice. It said to me that Ruth did not want to be at the orphanage. She wanted her mother. She had chosen me.

Evarista was in the front room. With determination, I told her I needed to talk about Ruth's health. Evarista was not disturbed; she acknowledged Ruth's condition, if obliquely. She told of visiting other orphanages before they opened La Casita. They all included at least some undernourished, sickly children. The women who started La Casita were determined that that would not be true of *their* orphanage. But it sometimes was. Some children simply wasted away with even the best of care. Those children they tried to place quickly. Colombian couples got first priority. In Ruth's case, there were no Colombian families that had all their papers in order, so she had been given to us. Evarista dug out of the office files a scrapbook of pictures of babies before and after adoption and pointed out scrawny babies transformed three months later into plump cherubs. Though the conversation was in English, and Evarista's English was fairly good, it sounded to me like something in a primitive language. The nuances were gone. I wondered if I grasped everything, if I had supplied connectives correctly, if I had unconsciously added what I wanted to hear. Ruth looked like a child abandoned on some Ethiopian wayside: that was the reality I saw. But Evarista's story was something to seize on, though I couldn't quite identify with it. At least it was something concrete I could tell Ken, and, in telling him, it might seem less like someone else's story and more like ours.

Ken arrived, distraught. He had found the lawyer's office. The lawyer had told him that something had gone wrong, but he had trouble figuring out what she was talking about. Someone, he deduced, who needed to sign something was out of town, and we would have to wait six days. Six days! Evarista called the lawyer and learned that we had to check back not in six days but at 6:00 P.M. The man—the only one in the city—who signed the passports was away. Then, at six, we learned that he would be away until the next day. We went back to the country club to wait.

That night I took a piece of string and measured exactly Ruth's position in her crib. I lined her up vertically and horizontally. The next morning I proved to my satisfaction that Ruth had moved about eight inches higher and a little bit toward the side. But she was moving. That was more than before, I was sure. At breakfast Sarah and Andrew claimed Ruth's neck seemed a lot stronger—it wasn't wobbling much at all.

Evarista called that morning to say the passport had been signed. But when Ken said we would try to get tickets to go to Bogotá, where we would get Ruth's visa, the next day, Evarista reminded him that Friday was the

Feast of the Assumption of the Blessed Virgin and that the whole country would probably close down, even the American Embassy in Bogotá. That meant we would have to wait until Monday to go to Bogotá, which meant we couldn't leave for home until Tuesday. I couldn't think past today. Ken could carry the burden of being upset this time. And he *was* upset. He decided to call the embassy to find out if there was any way we could clear Ruth's visa on Friday. "What about the separation of church and state?" he asked. The woman who did the visa work said she would ordinarily be glad to help, except that this particular Feast of the Assumption was her daughter's First Communion and the day would be taken up with the festivities.

The Taines were in the same situation. Resigned, Ken and Mat went off downtown to exchange money and to make plane reservations. I was left to care for Ruth and to do some chores. Every day I filled up my time boiling water, sterilizing bottles and nipples, making formula, washing diapers and clothes. One reason for the frequent washing was that only two blue stretch suits, both worn by Nicholas as a newborn, and one dress fit Ruth. Everything else accentuated her tininess, the skinniness of her arms and legs, and her bloated stomach.

The wash done, bottles ready to be used, I took Ruth out into the garden of the country club. She was so pale that I wanted her to get some sun. It was an idyllic day— sunny, seventy-five degrees, no humidity—one that made understandable Medellín's slogan, City of Eternal Spring. I showed Ruth the brilliant flowers and pointed out the birds thronging to the bird feeder, filled with scraps from the club's kitchen. I wanted her to respond to something. For Nicholas, looking was synonymous with grabbing. Not so for Ruth. She was still withdrawn—staring at things from a distance. But her crying at La Casita had marked a change. Now she could scream—with an intensity that made me panic. Ruth's wheezing and coughing had subsided since the day before, but she had not slept much that night. She began to fuss and, I decided, needed a nap. I would let her cry for twenty minutes, I promised myself, and then, if she hadn't stopped, I would pick her up. I returned to our room and put Ruth down. The crying started, and I went into the bathroom and closed the door. Time passed and the screaming continued. I sat there and wept, watching the minute hand on my watch creep forward and looking at the diapers and baby clothes hanging from every possible place in the bathroom. Twenty minutes passed, and Ruth's voice had not faltered in the least. I went in and picked her up. She had won, but she didn't stop crying. I had to hold her for more than an hour before she calmed down. Ruth could be awesome. I was both exhausted and a little impressed.

Ken and Mat returned with the air of conquerors: they had mastered, they claimed, the city, the country, the banking system, the airlines. Locked in the preholiday traffic of Medellín, they'd worried they wouldn't get to the bank before it closed. The one they chose first did not exchange dollars. They'd walked several blocks to another bank, which was guarded by men with machine guns. Mat did not have his passport and could not exchange any money. Ken cashed a fifty-dollar traveler's check for him. Then they'd gone to a ticket agent for Avianca. Ken had wanted to make reservations for our flight from Bogotá to Miami but learned that there was nothing we could get on Avianca for Tuesday. The agent had sent him to Braniff, around the corner. It all seemed perfect. We had a flight

to Bogotá for Sunday and one to Miami for Tuesday.
Now that we were staying longer than expected in
Medellín, we had time to go up the mountains to the
Antioquian plain to visit John and Carmela at their farm.
Carmela had come into town earlier in the week and on
hearing from Evarista that we were there had called and
urged us to come. I remembered remarking to a mother
who had adopted in Colombia that an advantage of such
an adoption was that one had an excuse to travel, that I
would be tempted to take extra time and see something
of Colombia. She had responded that the trip had not
been a vacation. The conversation haunted me. Here we
were in a gorgeous country, with time on our hands, being
given the opportunity by the Alfaros' invitation to see the
countryside without feeling like typical tourists—all of
which was a tourist's dream. But now I wanted only to get
home.

On Friday we made our way to the bus station. Ken
managed to figure out which was our bus, and we boarded
it before anyone else. Shortly after, it began to fill up.
Ruth, as I had feared, produced a very smelly diaper. I
managed to change her—balancing her on my lap—and
tried to submerge the dirty diaper in my sack in an unsuc-
cessful attempt to keep the smell from escaping into the
bus. No one, with the exception of Ken, seemed to notice.

We rocked up the steep mountainside in a bus decorated with crosses and icons of the Virgin. At times the
turns were so sharp, I found myself holding my breath.
Several times we passed broken-down or smashed buses
or cars. But the other passengers treated the trip matter-
of-factly. Halfway up the mountain, a little girl about four
threw up, twice, the second time all over the Adidas bag
of a young man standing in the aisle. The girl's mother

apologized and offered a towel to the young man, who wiped off his bag with remarkable good humor, I thought, although he edged a little farther away from the little girl.

The bus dropped us off in Rionegro, where we had been instructed to take a taxi. The town was small, built around a central square. The taxi drivers turned out to be locals who were willing to take people somewhere else for a fee. Six of us piled into an ancient Chevrolet and set off into the country. The land was flat, with mountains in the distance, and had a rugged, Wild West quality to it, albeit somewhat tamed. Ken commented that we were nearly five thousand feet above sea level. The farms along the way were neat and clean; whatever poverty there was at least wasn't evident on our route. In one little village all the people in the street or in the windows—the houses came right to the edge of the narrow street—were blond. Ruth was so fair; I wondered whether she was descended from these people.

About half an hour later the car left us off at the white stone wall that announced our friends' home, and we walked up the dirt road. We were in another world: three thousand miles from Nicholas, alone, in such a broad landscape, walking up a driveway to the ancient farmhouse ahead. Off to one side were bushes of large, intense red, orchidlike flowers. On the other side, a couple of whitewashed outbuildings in front of which a cow munched. Behind us, a long clean view of the plain under a few perfectly placed clouds.

Inside we found a comfortable house, U-shaped around a courtyard hanging with plants and Spanish moss. John and Carmela were, as always, gracious and warm. They exclaimed over Ruth. I had hoped that we could talk to them about Ruth's health, but I felt the same kind of oblique lack of contact as I had with Evarista at La Casita. Perhaps there was simply nothing they could say. We toured the buildings and gardens. For the fruit trees it was spring and summer together, the same trees bearing both blossoms and mature fruit. Lush vines of brilliant flowers climbed trellises. Coleus grew the size of large bushes. Even the cows in the small pasture beside the house were pristine. I was used to American farms with at least three abandoned, broken-down cars and trucks beside the barn. This farm looked unreal.

Soon after we got there, the Alfaros' daughter Angela arrived and suggested that we go horseback riding. Although the sky had begun to darken and Ken had never been on a horse, he agreed to go with her. I watched him mount what he was told was a gentle mare, stiffen his back, and follow Angela up the path toward the hills behind the house. Not an hour before, he had been complaining about how ill he felt. I was jealous of his ability to seize so readily a chance to escape from our state of illness and depression into adventure. I went with Carmela to look at her large and beautifully kept rose garden. Then it was time to feed Ruth. Carmela showed me the kitchen, and I boiled some water and gave Ruth a bottle. I changed her and washed out some clothes and diapers. Perhaps Ruth would sleep. It began to rain. Rain always made Nicholas sleep. Once he had slept a total of twenty-one hours in one day, and I had been so worried I had called the doctor. Nothing, of course, had been wrong.

Ken came in soaked and shivering. He said that the slow pace at the beginning hadn't lasted. The horse soon had broken into a trot and then a gallop that he had been certain would throw him. He'd done, he claimed, remarkably well until, on the way back, they galloped down the path to the farmyard and his horse, knowing the turn before he did, suddenly angled right and dumped him into a tree. He had survived it. He was quite triumphant.

Ruth woke up and we joined the Alfaros. We ate and talked for a couple of hours. I excused myself to feed Ruth and put her to bed—lying beside her to help her go to sleep. When I finally got up, the others were in front of the large fireplace in a room across the courtyard from where we had eaten. We talked about John's involvement in a school he'd established nearby, what their life was like in Colombia, their children, Ken's writing, Cervantes. I had taught *Don Quixote* for the first time that spring. John talked warmly about Don Quixote and Sancho, about the sadness of the book's ending. It was part of his life. I liked that. I felt that way about the book, but not in the intimate way John did. I envied him his Spanish, his culture. The austere, gracious, eighteenth-century Spanish farmhouse cast a spell. But pervading everything was my sense of nightmare—giving the loveliness of our surroundings a quality of the surreal. My cold made me feel unpleasant and ugly. I missed Nicholas. And my fear about Ruth pressed on me like a physical weight.

Ken had chills, but he was, nonetheless, vivacious, perhaps too much so. The Alfaros were concerned. John gave him a glass of rum. He decided to go to bed, and I said I had better, too, since Ruth had been waking up and crying a couple of times a night. Ken's illness seemed to me an emotional escape. If he was sick, he could retreat from everything.

The next morning Ken claimed he was a little better. We went back to Medellín on the bus and prepared to leave for Bogotá the following day. One last step to our trip and then we could go home to Nicholas and a doctor.

That next day we said our good-byes. We took pictures of the Taines, and they of us. We hugged them all and made plans to meet in Bogotá. Ruth, Sarah observed, had definitely put on weight and was carrying her head amazingly well. She *was* improving. I was afraid to believe it fully—but just maybe it was true. That weekend there was a swim meet at the country club for young teenagers, and we left in the midst of their hilarity.

Ken The flight to Bogotá was quick and easy. The plane skimmed low over Colombia's bare and open landscape. We seemed about to run into a range of mountains. There was no sign of a city. Then suddenly we landed. Bogotá appeared to be a long strip of skyscrapers backed by a mountain range. As soon as we were in the airport, a man approached us and offered his cab. I said yes, but once we were all loaded in the taxi, I was annoyed with myself. It was a gypsy. We should have found the official cabs and taken one of them. I prided myself on understanding how to get around cities.

To make matters worse, I was not confident of the address I gave the driver. Pat Smith back home had recommended that in Bogotá we stay in a particular *residencia* that specialized in putting up couples with adopted babies. Although she did not know the exact name of the place, she had assured me that I would be able to get a room and would not have to call ahead. While in Medellín, however, I had spent a couple of hours trying to track down the phone number. There had been no answer at any of the possible numbers I tried. Thus, I was relieved when the cab took us through a pleasant suburb of the city to the right address, although the fee the driver charged, I guessed, was higher than it should have been. At least the *residencia* actually existed. Susan stayed with Ruth in the taxi while I went to the door. I had been told that someone there spoke English. The maid who came to the door and peered suspiciously at me through the window said that the woman who knew English was not there. Another woman came to the door. What did I want? I tried to explain in my broken Spanish that we had come from Medellín with a baby from La Casita de Nicolás. I assumed that name would be known. The woman looked blankly at me. *"Adoptado,"* I said. She smiled. Could we have a room for two nights? No, the woman said, there was no room. The taxi driver appeared at my elbow, urging me to take the bags out of the cab so that he could be on his way. When he realized I did not have a reservation at the guesthouse, he suggested another place nearby. I didn't trust him. I turned back to the face at the door. I remembered the name of a doctor somehow connected with the place. I said the name. There was a pause. I didn't know whether the maid at the door simply caught a glimpse of Susan and Ruth in the car or whether my dropping the doctor's name had done the trick. All that mattered was the fact—the door opened. I paid off the driver and we went in.

As I was signing the register, Mrs. Andrade, the proprietress, returned. She did indeed speak English. Rich, obviously in charge, good-natured, and eccentric. Unlike the genteel women who ran La Casita, Mrs. Andrade was flashy. She wore orange hair and long strings of colored beads. She carried a Pekinese with her constantly and engaged in an endless conversation, or rather, often, a monologue. Exuding good will, she was like the president of a small, wealthy country whose only reason for being was to make people comfortable, and to make a little money on the side. She explained to us the system of the *residencia*. Water was always on the stove for sterilizing bottles and for making formula. Meals were served family style at seven, one, and seven. Second helpings and wine cost extra. Lunch was just about to be served. We dropped our bags. Susan changed Ruth. We went into the dining room. The meal was well prepared and delicious. We were lucky. I relaxed. After lunch, Susan organized our room, and even she seemed more at ease.

That evening at dinner Mrs. Andrade kissed and chatted briefly with all the guests. Besides Susan and me there were a French couple and a German couple, both adopting babies. They too had their babies with them. They were stocky, healthy-looking infants—half again Ruth's size, though we were told they were younger. As it turned out, Mrs. Andrade spoke French and German, as well as English and Spanish. We learned that the French woman had just arrived. Her husband had been in Bogotá a month and was about to return to France. The wife planned to stay for another month until the paperwork was completed and they could take their baby home. France, they said, made adoption in Colombia more difficult than did the States. There was also a table of American high-school students who had spent the summer in Colombia. The organization that had sponsored them was putting them up at this *residencia* for several days before their return to the States. They were full of their summer adventures and fascinated by the adopting parents and their babies. The adoption business surprised them. They had never imagined babies were hard to come by.

The proprietress made clear she would be helpful in

any way she could. I needed to change some money. She
directed me to her own bank, about a mile away, and
called ahead to be sure there'd be no problem. I left Susan
and Ruth napping and began to walk, thinking that would
be a good way to get a sense of the city. After a few minutes, however, I began to have difficulty breathing. Bogotá was, after all, more than eight thousand feet above sea
level. I was determined to act at home even in Bogotá, so
I stuck it out. Back at the *residencia,* Mrs. Andrade suggested we use her driver, Ernesto, to help us get around.

First thing Monday morning, Ernesto drove us to the
American Embassy, where I filled out a form detailing
Ruth's occupational, educational, and financial profile. I
wrote "baby" for her occupation. We left that and her
other papers. The petition for a visa, for which we'd ap-
plied in Philadelphia, had arrived. We were directed to
return in the afternoon for the visa itself. On the way out
we ran into the Taines, home away from home, and
confirmed our plans to meet later. Although Ernesto
spoke little English, he insisted on giving us a tour of the
city. I liked him. His English was about as good as my
Spanish. We worked as comrades to communicate.

Susan and I had talked about buying something
Colombian for Nancy, back home in Philadelphia with
Nicholas, and for Ruth herself. We decided we should do
it now. Ruth, in Susan's arms, was quiet, holding her hands
in front of her as she had that first evening at La Casita
or sucking her thumb. I realized how little I was tending
her. But I needed to look after the details of getting
places, doing the necessary things we had to do. And
Susan's turning her entire attention to Ruth helped cut
me off from both of them.

Ernesto took us to a couple of stores and then dropped

us downtown at the Taines' hotel. We had a drink with them. Susan and Sarah talked about our families' getting together for a week the next summer. The Taines suggested that they could rent a place near the Rhode Island cottage. I thought the idea sounded great. We had discovered that they actually lived in the same town, Andover, as Susan's sister Debby. Our lives were interconnected. We would be in touch. Outside, Ernesto was dozing in the car. We returned to the embassy and picked up Ruth's visa. Clockwork.

After supper I stopped by Mrs. Andrade's desk and asked her to confirm our reservation on the Tuesday-morning Braniff flight. Susan and I waited while she called. The stream of Spanish went on uncomfortably long. She hung up and said matter-of-factly that there was no reservation in our names. We would have to wait until Wednesday or maybe even later in the week. I exploded. What in God's name was going on! I'd been precise and careful when I made that reservation in Medellín. Mrs. Andrade was startled. Reservations made in Medellín were frequently ignored, she told me. What happened there was usually wrong anyway. Susan was crying. She was furious. It was impossible to stay another day. We had a son at home. Our daughter was sick. It was a shock to the woman, who picked up the phone and called the head of operations for Braniff in Bogotá. She got through immediately, talked for several minutes, and hung up, declaring she had worked things out. She had informed the chief of operations that a young American couple had to be on the Tuesday flight because they had a sick baby and there was an ambulance waiting at the airport in Miami. She obviously had pull and ingenuity. Someone else had been bumped from the flight.

The next morning Ernesto drove us to the airport, where our tickets were accepted and our luggage taken. I tipped him extravagantly, and we made our way to the overseas waiting room. The airplane left on time. Soon we would be home. I hoped Ruth wouldn't have too many diarrhea diapers en route. Susan thought she had a system for dealing with the formula. She'd filled up all our bottles with boiled water in Bogotá so that Ruth wouldn't have to get used to new water until the trip was over. The stewardess could heat up the water for the formula powder. The first try, however, just confirmed my suspicions of the Nestlé formula. The water the stewardess brought back was not hot enough to dissolve it. Ruth was crying in earnest. It promised to be a long trip.

Finally, in Miami we were moved with the other passengers onto a huge conveyor belt and into a room that turned out to be an elevator. This would be some people's introduction to the States. A system huge, impersonal, modern, strange—even to a native. We went through Customs and then followed the signs for Immigration, where Ruth's visa was processed without a hitch. One official was even unexpectedly solicitous, ushering us through before some other people. Strange how easily we agreed to bump people off flights, move ahead in line, take favors. The procedures seemed relatively simple until we got in line to book our Eastern flight. Eastern, again. I had left our ticket home open, since we had had no way of knowing when we would need a return flight. Now I learned that a plane for Philadelphia had just left. We would have to wait four hours for the next one. I was aggravated, but resigned. Somehow we'd get home. And Nicholas would be there.

We poked around the terminal looking for a comfortable place to wait. We ran into the group of American students from the *residencia*, wearing the hats and scarves and ponchos they'd acquired during the summer. A moment later, with delight, I spotted Mat Taine. The Taines had an hour to wait, so we all sat in a bar, weary, but reassured to have made contact again.

Ruth had been good for several hours, but now she was beginning to fuss. We needed to make some formula but had run out of Colombian water. Ruth was going to be introduced sooner than we hoped to American water. At least it wouldn't have to be boiled. Since tap water wouldn't be hot enough, Susan left Ruth with me and went to find some that would do. The Taines' new little boy recognized Ruth. He came around the table and poked her in a friendly way. I wondered what he was thinking. Ruth didn't show any signs of recognition, but, on the other hand, she was no longer fussing.

Susan returned about twenty minutes later, pleased with herself. She had chosen the most expensive looking restaurant that she could find in the terminal, explained her problem, and asked permission to go into the kitchen. There one of the cooks had given her a jar of nearly boiling water. She then took over the women's lounge connected to the restaurant and washed out bottles, nipples, and sundry wipe-up cloths. We were set until we got home. It was time for the Taines to leave. We were all certain that we would meet again soon.

Susan and I made our way to the waiting area for our flight, put Ruth on some blankets on the floor in one corner behind a bank of airport plastic seats, settled ourselves, and tried to rest. In an effort to relax, I bought a cigar. Several other people were smoking. The air was becoming heavy. Ruth was not sleeping. Finally, Susan gathered her up and went for a walk. By the time she returned, I had finished the cigar.

In what began to feel like a replay of our trip down, close to the time of our departure we were told that tornadoes south of us, where our plane originated, would delay our leaving. Time passed slowly. I got involved in a conversation with a woman from Philadelphia who was married to a Colombian and lived in Ecuador on a banana plantation. She led a rustic life without a phone or electricity and claimed to love it. It seemed a rather romantic existence, an escape, not at all like our own trip to Colombia. I could tell Susan was annoyed with me. I didn't understand why and chose to focus on passing the time. The night dragged on.

The Davenports and Nicholas were supposed to meet us in Philadelphia. Susan called to say that it looked like we might be as late as 4:30 A.M. Perhaps they would prefer not to come to the airport, or, at least, it might be better for them not to bring Nicholas. Susan seemed in favor of their letting him sleep. I wanted to know what harm there could be in Nancy's getting Nicholas up. She wanted to see Nicholas as much as I did, Susan responded, but Nicholas was going to have a lot to adjust to when we got home. We shouldn't add to it a bad night's sleep. Also, Susan added, she felt uncomfortable urging Nancy to come to the airport in the middle of the night with a seven-month-old. We should be more flexible. We owed the Davenports a lot. I felt it was unfair of her to insist on gratitude at such a time. We were dealing with enough as it was. We dealt with things in silence awhile. The point was, Nicholas was fine, Nancy had said.

The flight from Miami to Philadelphia was surreal. Ruth hadn't slept for more than a couple of hours in nearly twenty. She was exhausted. We were exhausted. She lay across our laps on a pillow. Our money was about gone, although I found enough to buy a beer. Occasionally, Ruth cried out. Susan slept fitfully. The cabin was dark, but outside the lights from the airplane reflected on the clouds created a psychedelic play of color that suggested we had entered another world. For a moment, half asleep, dreaming, I believed we had been transported to Venus.

When we arrived in Philadelphia at 4:30 A.M., not only Bill Davenport but our friends Linda and Ward Stanley were there at the gate. I was surprised and moved. Nancy was waiting outside in the car with Nicholas. I would be seeing him in just a few minutes. We were really home. We made our way through the terminal, collected our bags, and went outside. Nicholas, sleepy and bewildered, was sitting in his baby seat in the car. He was huge, and Chinese! I was shocked by my reaction. Susan was hugging Nicholas. I touched him tentatively. We all had to get to bed. The Stanleys, whose house was near ours, drove us and the babies home. The Davenports would drop off Nicholas's equipment the next day.

We had been superstitious enough not to leave the house set up for two babies. So now we put Nicholas back in his room and created a makeshift arrangement for Ruth in ours. We slept for a couple of hours. Then, at 9:30 in the morning, we packed up both babies and took them to the pediatrician's office. Simply seeing an American doctor signaled to me the beginning of a return to normalcy. Food and home could make all the difference in the world, she reassured us. Judging from Ruth's weight—ten pounds—and her development, she believed she was several months younger than the age given us. Both Susan and I were sure La Casita had given us her correct birth date. Ruth's diarrhea, the doctor felt, was to be expected, given the change in her life and diet. To be on the safe side, however, she recommended that every few days for a couple of weeks we take a stool sample to the Public Health Department to be tested for parasites. She didn't have a clear idea what would happen to Ruth's distended stomach. She thought "sillygas" was possibly an antacid and/or laxative. Stomachs bloated from malnutrition, she felt, were not dealt with that easily. For me the name "sillygas" had said it all.

As concerned as I was for Ruth, I felt pulled away by Nicholas, who was fidgeting on my lap. Nicholas's hands and feet were so large compared with Ruth's. I had trouble feeling connected to him. Nicholas had not slept well when we had all gone to bed that morning, and he'd refused to eat anything when we'd gotten him up. He wasn't the baby I remembered. Susan was trying to get the doctor to give a more concrete, if tentative, analysis of Ruth's condition. She might well be fine, said the doctor, though of course even if she improved drastically, it would take a while before the real impact of her first five and a half months could be determined. Right now it was impossible to tell whether there would be any scars. For the time being she thought it best to postpone all of Ruth's shots until she was stronger. Susan stressed how much Ruth had changed in the eleven days we'd had her. Her neck was much stronger. She was beginning to move in the crib. She had discovered her feet. The doctor said all that sounded good. We made an appointment for a few days later and went home. If Ruth didn't improve radically soon, we agreed to take her for a full exam to specialists at Children's Hospital.

RUTH

Susan and I had a lot to do to arrange the room that was to be shared by both babies. We prepared to move into what had been Nicholas's room. It was blisteringly hot. August in Philadelphia at its worst. Much too hot to move all the books and arrange the furniture. So we did the minimum, piling books up in the hall to put in place later. The babies were demanding—Nicholas as much as Ruth. Obviously at seven months he was not too young to be jealous. I dug out of the storage closet the infant seat long ago relinquished by Nicholas. We placed Ruth in it on the floor with toys around her, while we tried to organize the house. Nicholas was fascinated by Ruth, as an object to grab and poke. She stared at him solemnly, while he zoomed around with his well-mastered crawl. He seemed twice her size. We dubbed them the Sumo and the Waif.

Susan's concern about Ruth soon developed a new focus. After checking up on several of Ruth's symptoms in Dr. Spock, she became convinced that Ruth had cystic fibrosis. I woke up in the middle of the night to find her, crying, standing by Ruth's crib. To her the disease clearly fit. Ruth had respiratory and digestive problems, and she was an obvious "failure-to-thrive" baby. I reasoned that if she felt that concerned, she should call the doctor in the morning and ask her directly about it. The doctor didn't understand Ruth, Susan responded. Why did she have to mention "scars"? Weren't there any doctors in the city who were authorities on this kind of baby, babies from foreign orphanages? She even wondered how helpful it would be to take Ruth's stool samples to the Health Department for testing. Did they understand South American parasites? I reminded her that we could always take Ruth to Children's Hospital and track down a specialist.

Why put her through tests if they weren't necessary? Susan objected. Well, no matter what, I pleaded, we had to get some sleep. Tomorrow was to be my first day back at the office. And certainly one or both babies would be waking up within an hour or two.

The next morning I dressed to leave for work. Even though the first days after a vacation were always nerve-racking, I looked forward to my office. I felt I'd been in something of a daze the last couple of weeks, unsure of what was happening and would happen. My job was a welcome reality. Downstairs, however, I found Susan trying to feed the babies breakfast in the kitchen, sobbing as she did so, and I angrily said that I'd stay home. Her immediate and genuine gratitude made me at once sympathetic. It would be hard to manage the babies alone. Actually, I believed Susan capable of handling anything she wanted, but she clearly didn't feel she had control now. And I couldn't tell what would make the difference. Ruth's health concerned me, too, but Susan's depression was difficult for me to understand. She was worried enough for both of us. Debby and her son were coming for a few days soon. That would be a help.

Right after breakfast Susan left a message with the doctor, and I called our friend Tom Goodman and asked him if he would stop by and translate Ruth's medical record. Maybe that would give us some understanding of her condition. Tom stopped by and deciphered what he could of her record. The handwriting of Colombian doctors was similar, he complained, to that of their U.S. colleagues. Ruth had had bronchitis several times. There was something in the record about a skin problem. She'd had most of the normal shots. Nothing extraordinary.

Mary, Nicholas's neighborhood grandmother, dropped

by to see "Nicholas's new sister." I could see Susan was determined to be positive. Mary should just see how much Ruth had improved since we picked her up! Clearly upset, Mary asked if we had had to take her. She said she'd pray for Ruth and picked up and cuddled Nicholas. He, as always, was delighted to see her.

The doctor returned Susan's call. Susan asked about cystic fibrosis. From her voice I judged that calling the doctor was the right thing to do. She reported when she hung up that although the doctor said she couldn't positively eliminate that disease, she didn't believe it was likely. Embarrassed, Susan admitted she'd been afraid to kiss Ruth ever since she read that one sign of the disease was the high sodium chloride content of the sweat. She'd feared she would discover Ruth's sweat was excessively salty. The doctor told her that taste was not a reliable indicator. I took Susan's chagrin as a good sign.

The incredibly hot days continued. It was hard to do anything more than meet the most basic needs. With guilt and relief, I went back to work. The crises of my job were for the most part expected and manageable. And I was, for the moment, a celebrity returned with a baby from the heart of Latin America. Debby and her son arrived. While they were there, I could leave for the office with an easier conscience.

We talked frequently about the Taines. How were they doing with their new son? Sarah would be pleased by Ruth's progress. We told Debby about them. She and Dennis, we thought, would enjoy them. Far away in Colombia, we had met a family who lived practically in her neighborhood. Debby said she'd get in touch with them when she went back home. She would report on Ruth and her visit to Philadelphia.

A few days after leaving, Debby phoned us. She sounded upset. She had called the Taines. Sarah had told her they no longer had a new son. They had given up their parental rights. Debby hadn't known what to say.

I couldn't believe it. Susan was in a state of shock. She knew Sarah better than I. What on earth could have happened? Susan telephoned Sarah immediately.

Sarah, it seemed, had had some kind of nervous collapse immediately on coming home. She had had a severe postpartum depression after their biological baby had been born eight years before. Something similar seemed to have happened with the arrival of this child. It all sounded strange to me. Susan was devastated. As she put it, the one contact we'd had with the reality we'd experienced in Colombia was now gone. She thought *she* was having a hard time. Sarah must have been going through hell. Why hadn't Sarah phoned? How little we knew them. We felt alone, deserted.

Ironically, although my camera worked well enough before and after the trip, all the pictures I took in Colombia turned out as dark, damaged images—as if light had leaked into the camera. The contact sheets were something of an icon of the entire trip: partial images, dark frames, lost experiences. We knew the place existed and that people were there. We had been there and seen them. But that "objective" record of meeting Ruth and her first days with us, which I, at least, wanted for Ruth and for us, was gone.

Ruth's diarrhea continued for several weeks, but no parasites were found. And her appetite in that time became good and then extraordinary. She began drinking eight eight-ounce bottles of formula and eating three meals a day. Susan worried it was unnatural, a symptom of some disease. Cystic fibrosis remained a cloud over our heads, but it soon became obvious that Ruth's weight gain and growth were as exceptional as her appetite. Her weekly doctor's visits revealed that she was gaining about a pound and a half and growing about an inch a week. There was still an intensity about her as she sat on the floor, studying the rattle she was so fond of. Nicholas raced around, stealing toys, bopping her, and, occasionally, simply watching her. She continued to want a lot of physical contact. Susan would hold and rock her several hours a day. She was becoming, nonetheless, an extremely easy baby. In Colombia we said how nice it would be if Ruth turned out to have Nicholas's wonderful temper and perfect sleeping and eating habits. And that is what happened. Ruth became her own version of the baby Nicholas had been. Evarista had been right. There was nothing wrong with Ruth physically. Her "failure-to-thrive" had emotional roots. In a remarkably short time in our home she was transformed. She became downright plump. I was convinced Ruth was going to be a strong child, a strong woman. I liked that.

Nicholas, on the other hand, was no longer an easy baby. If our backs were turned for a moment, he would clamber onto the tray of his high chair, stand up, and throw all of his food across the kitchen. He had become contrary about eating. And he stopped sleeping through the night. I was surprised when one evening I discovered that Susan's response to Nicholas when she first saw him in the backseat of Nancy's car had been similar to mine. He looked gigantic. And somehow she hadn't thought about his being Chinese. Odd as it seemed, until that moment we hadn't fully grasped, on an emotional level, that Nicholas was racially different from us. When we came back from Colombia, we needed to get to know not one baby, but two. That, at least for me, was the ultimate shock of the trip.

Soon, however, I again felt close to Nicholas. Nicholas with his extraordinary curiosity about everything, his delight at his own accomplishments, his chortles over his favorite nursery rhyme, "A farmer went riding on a gray mare—bumpity, bumpity, bump." At times even his clear jealousy of Ruth drew me to him. His waking at night, nonetheless, began to drive me crazy. I didn't agree with Susan's solution—getting up and rocking him for an hour. I was afraid we were encouraging a pattern that he would never break. Susan insisted that she needed some time alone with Nicholas. Any thoughts that infertility was the great test of our life together and after that everything would be easy had been naive, to say the very least.

Gradually, however, we created a pattern that worked. Susan's school was in session. Dinnie came in several days a week to look after the babies and to do some housekeeping. I left late for work two mornings. Susan was home the other mornings and two afternoons. We would both race home, anxious to be with the babies.

Nicholas and Ruth were clearly becoming, for all intents and purposes, twins. One night, when Susan and I checked them before going to bed, we couldn't find Ruth. After a moment of panic, we noticed a sleepy head poking out from under Nicholas's crib. Part of Ruth's bed had broken. Without a whimper, she had crawled out and over to Nicholas. The two were developing a primitive language with each other. We would hear them jabbering in their room long after they were put down to sleep. We listened to them together, aware of the changed and extended bond between us.

I thought of how I had once pictured myself. A young professional for whom children were unnecessary. That was a lifetime away. The one worry Susan and I had had about having children was that it would affect how we felt about each other. It had. We were less of a simple unity, but more richly entwined. I had no desire to go back.

In early winter, Susan arranged that the whole family visit Dan Meyer late one Friday afternoon, after his usual office hours. He was delighted with the visit and the babies. Susan promised she'd send him a picture of the two of them just as they were then, sitting in their twin stroller, to put in his file. We were no longer an infertile couple.

It was important to me that the children be baptized. I half expected Susan to object, but she didn't. It was to be at Pentecost, June 1982. The babies were almost a year and a half. My parents and sister Karen drove up from Virginia. Debby and her family drove down from Massachusetts. It would be a gathering of most of the people who had been involved in our battle and search for our children. People like Frances Davies, who had so empathized with Susan's infertility. Bonnie Klein, who had first told us about La Casita de Nicolás. John and Carmela Alfaro. Mary Pearson, our children's next-door grandmother. Tom Goodman, our official Spanish translator. Most of our close friends, like Peter and Peshe, Linda and Ward, Susan's women's group, people from my office. Even Celeste and Nat Berger, who had actually put Nicholas in our arms.

I wrote a psalm for the occasion. It was arranged, in fact, that I would read it as part of the service. I started, but my usual stage presence was overwhelmed by our two children, by the immensity of what they had brought us.

Frank Griswold, the priest, came up to the lectern and gently took the poem from me. I rejoined Susan, Nicholas, and Ruth in the front pew. Ruth wiggled into my lap. Frank began reading where I had stopped:

> *These children, drawn by desire,*
> *step from enormity toward us;*
>   *a Red Sea shuts behind them.*
>
> *They arrive:*
> *the air is changed in their coming.*
> *We are changed in seeing them.*

Susan gave my arm a caress. Nicholas linked his arm in mine and, in a posture so characteristic of him, leaned against me.

※ Epilogue: Real Parents

We all assume that we are fertile and potential parents. The intensity of the feelings occasioned by infertility, the uneasy reactions to those problems one sees in people who do not have them, and the emotions evoked by adoption all attest to the significance of that assumption. But if infertility threatens the identity of the fertile, how much more it can take over the identity of the infertile. I look back on that period of trying unsuccessfully to have children as a time when my personality was warped. I saw the world through different glasses. Fertility was, for me, not only at the heart of being a woman but, also, of being a creative, productive human being. Infertility was deathlike.

I remember at one time refusing to think about why I wanted my Ph.D., because I was afraid I'd discover something that would make me not want to go after it. Similarly, I resisted thinking about why I was reluctant to adopt, because I was afraid I'd discover something that would make me see bearing a child physically as no better than adopting one. I didn't want to give up believing adoption was only "second best."

I saw a biological baby as an acknowledgment of my creativity. I infused a physical happening with symbolic meaning. If I had borne a child physically, I might have been sorely disappointed when I found that a pregnancy did not magically define me forever as a "creative person." I also thought of having a child through adoption, rather than pregnancy, as giving up a certain power—that of being literally everything to someone, if only for nine months. The need for that kind of power, when I articulate it as I have now, seems suspect—an echo of the impossible desire to be at the center of the world, to be omnipotent.

It took me a long time to come to terms with infertility. But in the end it has come to mean simply a missed experience, and, I know, very few people have all the major experiences they want in a lifetime. Motherhood continues to be a key for me to feeling creative, but I finally understand that being a mother is different from producing a baby. The last and probably most important reason for my original fear of adoption was that I didn't fully grasp that. I didn't think through to the fact that I love my parents because they mothered me and fathered me, not because I have their genes. That I am grateful to my mother not because she carried me for nine months— about that I feel surprisingly neutral—but because she loved me.

As our story makes clear, Ken and I did not simply decide one morning to look into adoption. We tried on the idea for months—years—and gradually grew into it. And often our emotional change was preceded by experiences that pushed us to change.

At the beginning, since adoption was a way of doing what we had been trying to do physically, the younger the baby was and the more he or she physically resembled us, the more it felt like the original impulse. Jonathan, a new-born Caucasian baby from middle-class parents, who even looked like us, seemed the ideal. Our experience with him remains a touchstone for us. We continue to feel that we lost our first child. Many people have indicated, often obliquely, that they cannot understand the intensity of that feeling. "You never saw the baby," they point out. We know that is mercifully true. It could have been much worse, although at the time that did not seem possible. People have also reminded us that the baby did not die. Again, that is literally true. In another sense, our loss was nonetheless a death: a life was taken from us as finally as death takes life. Certainly, we experienced the grief that follows death. Ken and I still regret the decision Jonathan's biological mother made, because we believe it was not in his best interest nor, of course, in ours; nevertheless, we feel uneasy condemning her decision to retain her parental rights. Ours, we know, is a one-sided story, but that does not take away our loss.

The most important consequence, although we could not see it at the time, was that we emerged from the event committed in a way that we had not been before to adoption as a form of childbearing. We began to think of ourselves as parents. After all, we did have a child, if only briefly, and the means by which we bore that child made no difference in our feelings of attachment or loss. After Jonathan, we found that the assumption we shared with so many people—that adoption was second best—had vanished. We knew better—if only by the measure of our grief.

But not only did Jonathan help us experience the fact that bonding is not determined by biological connection; he also contributed to the gradual change in our feelings about our child's ethnic identity. If the biological bloodline was not necessary to identify our child, then ethnic differences became less of a concern. They were important for a child's identity, certainly, but not for the bond one had with one's child. And it was for that bond—the experience of giving ourselves, our backgrounds, our values, of intimately witnessing the growth of another human being, and, most important, of being loved and loving—that we wanted to be parents.

Nonetheless, ethnic, racial difference is not something, it seems to me, to be taken lightly. And it's not something that is "resolved" or understood completely at any one time. Before Nicholas was born, we were certainly aware that our baby would be racially different from us, and after he was with us, we enjoyed his being Chinese. But still, that attribute didn't seem particularly relevant. Possibly he didn't look particularly Oriental. But, more important, a tiny baby—it seems to me in retrospect—is so dependent and, as a result, is such an extension of self that it is hard to appreciate him fully as a separate, distinct being. Whatever the reason, when we returned from Colombia, Ken and I both feel we fell in love with Nicholas a second time. And this time it was different. His being Chinese was inextricably connected to him. His almond eyes, his straight, fine black hair that stuck straight up (a Chinese Afro, we called it), his pale olive skin, were part of what made him our Nicholas. He has become our "Oriental tyrant"—a child whose will is equaled only by his extraordinary charm. He is a magical child: delighted by life, ornery, inquisitive, affectionate, impossible. His being

Chinese seems a minor characteristic, but without it, he wouldn't be our Nicholas. There will, of course, be changes in the future in at least how he understands his racial origins and possibly in how we do. In that we will follow his cue—as all parents must in dealing with their children's developing sense of identity.

Nicholas is not what we expected eleven years ago when we started trying to have children—but more wonderful than we dreamed possible. The same can be said about Ruth. I remember how strange I found that conversation with the mother of the Chilean child who remarked that in a way she and her husband felt lucky their daughter was so far behind developmentally when they got her. They didn't miss any stage in her growth. Yet now I can identify with that mother. Ruth's failure to thrive those first five and a half months before we brought her home allowed us to witness all the stages of her development—as we had Nicholas's.

Ruth was our daughter come what may, and just as parents can't prescribe—however much they would like to—the health of a biological child, we couldn't prescribe Ruth's condition. There are solid psychological (as well as practical) reasons why agencies, not prospective parents, decide on which babies should go to which couples. Biological parents have some controls over the child they produce that adopting parents don't have, and adopting parents have controls that biological ones don't. But, ultimately, for adopting parents their child is no more a possession to be chosen from a lineup than is the child of biological parents. There are no guarantees; babies are the embodiments of unknowns. Problems, however, can create bonds. In a sense I feel that I gave my daughter the will to live. And I love her for allowing me that power.

Holding and rocking Ruth for several hours a day provided me with an experience, I now see, that I myself needed. It was something like being pregnant, with the added advantage of being consciously willed by child as well as mother. The winter Ruth turned one, she would insist on my unbuttoning my sweater and closing it around her, so that she was held snugly against me, wrapped in the same woolen cocoon. By the time she turned two, she had outgrown the need to be so held and rocked. I felt both satisfied and a little sad.

Ruth has become a child quite the opposite of what seemed to be promised by the passive, distant baby we first held in our arms. Her early development *was* different from the normal pattern. At fourteen months, even though she crawled well, she still could not turn over from her back to her stomach. I had just started to look into the possibility of physical therapy, when one day Ruth suddenly rolled over. The next day she walked. After that she quickly became one of the most active and outgoing children on the playground. Once when Ruth was about two, another mother watched her zoom up and down the jungle gym, up and down the slide, clamber onto the rocking horse, half topple off, and dash back to the slide. "How do you manage her at home?" the mother asked me. "I feel sorry for you." I laughed with pleasure at the question. Ruth became a child who for a while was dubbed on the playground Little Florence Nightingale. If another child started to cry, she'd race over and hug the child—much to his or her surprise. At three she announced that the stray cat in the backyard whom she befriended was named Comfort.

The infertile who want children frequently feel a lack of sympathy from those around them—both before they decide to adopt and after. Some people tend to see adoption as an easy option and to condemn someone for not looking into it, for not immediately wanting to adopt an older child, or one who is biracial, from another country, or even handicapped: if you are not parochial, if you really want to be a parent, they feel, then you shouldn't have any problem thinking about almost any kind of adoption. At the beginning of our adoption investigation, Kathryn, the mother who had adopted through the Cradle Society, advised us not to compromise in the kind of child we wanted. That remains advice with which I fully agree. Thinking about adoption requires being honest with yourself, accepting yourself. It is a process that is intensely private, a process that, from the outside, can be difficult to understand.

Ken and I may have felt condemned at times for having a problem with the idea of adoption. But once that difficulty disappeared, we felt at times *equally* misunderstood. The sympathy I received after my miscarriage was immediate and from everyone—in a way it was not from everyone after losing Jonathan. Both losses were terrible, but for me one was an early miscarriage and the other a stillbirth, and in the usual hierarchy of losses, the latter is worse. That the loss of Jonathan was a stillbirth, however, was hard for some people to grasp.

It is because adoption is like birth—an experience that puts you in touch with your endurance, your fear, your capacity for joy—that couples in the process are so emotionally vulnerable and can so easily fall prey to an anxiety that approaches paranoia. In retrospect, much of our anxiety about losing Nicholas seems unnecessary, especially once we had him in our home. The impending arrival of the social worker, for example, certainly caused more anxiety than it should have. We had been through homestudies and knew reasonably well what they were like. But having Nicholas—falling in love with him, knowing that emotionally he could not have been more ours if we had physically borne him, yet the city had more legal claim to him than we—made us paranoid. We assumed for a while that every person involved in finalizing the adoption would be looking for ways to take him from us—which, of course, was not true.

But there were so many things that could go wrong. Our experience with Jonathan made us acutely aware of that. Having children is emotionally packed for biological mothers as well as adopting mothers. And, in fact, we found out later, there *were* hitches in what happened with Nicholas. We were lucky his birth relatives were so secure, so strong.

First, soon after the biological mother returned home from the hospital, she received from a private photographer a folder of full-color photographs of the newborn Nicholas, taken shortly after birth. There were fifty prints—a special gift for the new mother at a low, low price. She was urged to take this unique opportunity to carry forever in her heart and wallet that precious first image of her child. Fortunately, the girl's mother immediately shipped the photographs back to the Bergers, who returned them with a sharp admonishing note to the hospital, which, it turned out, was not aware of this particular photographer's activities.

Second, we found out several months later that the reason we had to wait so long for Nicholas that first night was not a problem with his circumcision. His biological grandmother had decided to crochet a suit for him—her last gift. It was not finished by the scheduled time, and she insisted that the Bergers wait until she completed it. Celeste and Nat sat there, watching that woman crochet an outfit the child she would never see again would never wear. We assume that the Bergers still have that suit. We believe that eventually it should be Nicholas's. It is now almost four years later, and we know Nicholas is our child, but we are ambivalent about having it. For me that suit is simply—right now—too potent an image of the emotional depths, and thus the vulnerability, of both Nicholas's birth relatives and of Ken and me, his parents.

Nicholas's final hearing, externally, at least, seemed pro forma. More recently we have been told of several cases in which the biological mother regained custody after the Voluntary Relinquishment. Fortunately, we had not heard of them until after our wait was over. We have also become aware of a couple of cases in which the biological parents regained custody even after the final decree. We do not allow ourselves to think about that.

Except for odd moments, our paranoia is gone. We have our children. At times, recently, I've almost felt a bit tired of the subject of adoption. To the teachers at their school, to our families, to our friends, to their friends, to us, to them, Nicholas and Ruth aren't our adopted children; they are our children. Nonetheless, occasionally I find in myself a residual, more generalized insecurity.

One afternoon when I arrived at Nicholas's and Ruth's preschool to pick them up, I saw Nicholas hanging from a bar of the jungle gym. I went up to him, prepared for his usual squeal of pleasure when he saw me. "Go away," he told me. "You're not my mother. You're someone else's." "Whose mother am I?" I asked slowly, stalling for time to steady myself. "Ruth's," he answered. That was some relief: at least both of my children weren't being taken away from me. And the absurdity of that thought made me realize with pain that I saw myself as vulnerable because I was an adoptive mother. The next instant, I simply didn't care whether I was or wasn't adoptive. I could no more stop being his mother than stop life itself. "I'm Nicholas's mother," I said. "Who are you?" "I'm a monkey," he answered. "Can't you tell?!" And he dropped from the bar and scampered away.

It is so easy for parents who have adopted to assume that their children's need to separate themselves from them, to form their own identity, is somehow unique to their children. What characterizes all children is interpreted as a reflection on adoption. Actually, it may not be that adoptive parents are really more insecure than nonadoptive parents, but simply that they have such a clear focus for normal, everyday parental insecurity.

But if they are more insecure, it stems from something in which all or almost all of us in our society inevitably participate. In one very specific way, whether we like it or not, Ken and I have been changed not simply by our experience of having children, but by having adopted them. We are sensitive to things we never noticed before. Some years ago if someone had said to me that there is a profound prejudice in our society against adoption, I think—I'm afraid—that I would have dismissed him. Now that perception is something that at times I feel bombards me.

Several years ago, when my interest in adoption led me to do some reading in the sociological and psychological literature, I discovered that adoption is generally seen as something negative—at best, a condition to be overcome. It is commonly accepted, for example, that a disproportionate number of adopted people exhibit

abnormal behavior and seek psychiatric help or are insti-
tutionalized. It is only fairly recently that studies have
questioned the statistical soundness of such assumptions.
The major reason why so much research has shown adoption in such a negative light is that, typically, nonadopted
people have been compared with adopted people who
were undergoing some psychiatric care. The view that
adoptive status brings stress to the individual, to quote a
current researcher, Leslie Stein, has been largely "drawn
from the clinical data of writers who have attempted to
account for the existence of *pathology* in their clinical
patients." Stein's study, recently published by the Child
Welfare League, is one of only three studies so far—
and the literature on adoption, I must add, could fill a
library—in which adopted adolescents from a nonclinical
population are compared with parallel nonadoptive
adolescents. Her examination of ninety-one white middle-class adolescents reveals no significant difference in
the strength of identity between adopted and nonadopted teenagers. The study hardly seems surprising.
What is surprising is that the results are considered a
discovery of new material.

One day not so long ago, Ken came home from work
unusually upset. An author had come by to discuss a book
proposal with him—a fairly ordinary occurrence. It
turned out that her thesis was a support of the triangular
concept of adoption, which argues that, in all adoptions,
all three parties—the birth parents, the child, and the
adoptive parents—should know each other. It made him
a bit uncomfortable, he told me, but he felt it was a normal enough concept and, if the author supported it intelli-
gently, could make a book. As the meeting went on,
however, it became clear her stance was not objective:

she had "given up her baby," had never recovered from it, had never forgiven herself for "cutting him off from his roots." It was clear that to her the birth mother was the real mother, the adoptive parents simply caretakers. It was hard for Ken to remain calm, but he managed to survive the encounter, telling her finally that the book didn't sound quite right for an academic press. She should write a couple of sample chapters and try commercial publishers. He never mentioned he was an adoptive father.

There is no way—at this point—that Ken and I can avoid feeling threatened by those people who propound explicitly that the birth parent is the real parent, the only anchor for a child's identity. And that thesis is at the moment highly visible. Not so long ago, while waiting for my appointment in a doctor's office, I opened *Newsweek*. Lorraine Dusky's "My Turn" caught my eye. Dusky argues that a child who lacks contact with his "natural heritage by adoption" is at some level a "troubled one." "For years," she writes, "I've collected bits of data about certain unfortunate people in the news: Son of Sam, the Hillside strangler, the Pennsylvania shoemaker who raped and brutalized several women, a Florida man who killed at least 34 women, the man sought in connection with the Tylenol scare. All of them grew up not knowing at least one of their natural parents: most knew neither." The absurdity of her "evidence," her "logic," is startling. Still, her formulation is only an extreme example of a common tendency. If adoption is assumed to be a negative state and an adopted child has problems of one sort or another, it's quite understandable to associate adoption with those difficulties. The evidence, however, to support the idea that being adopted makes one's life difficult is produced by the very assumption that it does. If a person who happens to have been adopted is adjusted and successful, that fact about his or her upbringing is something we rarely know. When we find it out, it is similar to finding out that someone is a twin—an interesting deviation from the norm. But not so if a person has difficulties. I once heard a student's problems "explained" by the fact that he was adopted.

What bothered me even more than Dusky's article was the fact that it was *Newsweek* I was reading, a middle-of-the-road, popular newsmagazine that was slanted in a way generally acceptable to millions of Americans and that didn't publish statements, even in the section "My Turn" (written by someone new each issue), that seemed preposterously off-the-wall. The same issue had an article on infertility. It gave one paragraph to adoption, the final "resort" of "thousands of infertile couples." "Some couples who do adopt," I read, "claim they are just as fulfilled as they would have been with a child of their own." To the ears of a mother who happens to have adopted, "some" and "claim" suggest doubt: that adopting a child is as fulfilling as having one biologically is an opinion, perhaps even a self-deluded opinion, held by only some people. And that implication is echoed in the way the sentence ends. As long as only a biological child is a child "of one's own," as long as an adopted child is *really*, when all is said and done, "someone else's," then of course it's a delusion to think that adopted children are as fulfilling as biological children.

Probably nothing more clearly reveals the unconscious attitudes toward adoption than the language that is commonly used to denote different aspects of it. The phrase "put out a child for adoption" implies that giving up parental rights is unfeeling, mechanical. A child is being put out of the house, cut off, discarded. "Put up for adoption" actually uses the same verb idiom as "put up for sale." The connotations of those words lead inevitably to other adoption words. People normally speak of the biological mother as the "real mother" or "natural mother" and biological children as "children of one's own." In the last four years I have many times been asked if Nicholas and Ruth were my "real children," my "own children." I'm sure I used those phrases in the past, but now, in spite of their familiarity, they bite deeply. What do those words imply about the adoptive parents? That they are not the real parents but just playing at being parents, just pretending to be the parents of their children? Nicholas and Ruth are not my and Ken's "own children," just our pretend children? The biological mother is the natural one; the adoptive mother is unnatural? People who are not consciously opposed to adoption in any way use highly charged language, assuming all the while that they are using neutral, objective words.

The philosopher Judith Jarvis Thomson, in her well-known, frequently anthologized essay "A Defense of Abortion," notes that though she would argue against "the right to secure the death of the unborn child," she has sympathy for the "woman [who] may be utterly devastated by the thought of a child, a bit of herself, put out for adoption and never seen or heard of again" and who may "therefore want not merely that the child be detached from her, but more, that it die." What does that imply? A child's essential identity is that of being "a bit" of the mother's "self." Adoption means throwing a child out into the cold, bleak world to grow up motherless, undefended. An adoptive mother, from that perspective, cannot be a real mother, and a child has no more independent identity than the hair trimmed from one's head. At a recent colloquium on adoption, Ken heard a woman speak of her experience talking to high-school students about adoption. The prevalent attitude among young nonadopted girls, she said, was that they would never be so unnatural as to give up for adoption any babies they might have. They would much prefer aborting. Belief in adoption does not necessarily mean denying the option of aborting. There are carefully reasoned arguments for abortion. But it is difficult to see any way to make logical the argument that if a woman doesn't want or can't bring up a child, abortion is the only alternative *because* it would be cruel or uncaring and unnatural to give up her parental rights to another couple. It is not unnatural to ensure that a child is mothered and fathered by caring people. Still, those young girls are just making explicit the prejudice implied when biological parents are referred to as the "natural" parents.

If someone using the words "real" or "natural" to describe birth parents is challenged, he or she might claim, of course, that nothing is meant by that. It is just a figure of speech. Alternative phrases like "give up parental rights," "biological mother," "birth parents," "bioparents," often seem unidiomatic, or at least forced. Yet if there is one thing we have learned in the last twenty years, it is that language does indeed carry cultural assumptions. It is seldom neutral. What we say reflects what we think. Changing assumptions often requires that the language itself change—and that is seldom comfortable.

The first days of my children's preschool I found myself fielding numerous questions from other parents who, like me, were curious about which children belonged to which parents and who thus were mystified by Nicholas and Ruth. They were the same age—were they both mine? Were they twins? When I explained to one mother that they were adopted, she remarked with a half laugh, half sigh that she wished she could say that about her son; he'd been extremely difficult recently. Later, in another conversation when I again explained Nicholas and Ruth were adopted, another mother responded warmly that that didn't matter, that caring for children after they were born was much more important than giving them birth. When I mentioned this last incident to Peshe, she likened it to telling someone she was Jewish and being told that didn't matter, other things were more important. The prejudice is there—but only to sensitized ears. One thing I find upsetting is how easy it is for me, like most people, to be insensitive unless the experience is my own.

One adoptive mother told us that she was so excited about her baby and that it was so miraculous that she and her husband had actually been able to adopt him that at first when people remarked about him, she would proudly tell them he was adopted. The two most common responses she received seem to me to summarize quite succinctly, though more obviously than most of us would express ourselves, basic societal attitudes about adoption. The first response was "What kind of mother would give up such a beautiful baby!" The second, "Oh, what a good Christian you are!" (The fact that she happened to be Jewish gave that last comment a little extra punch.)

Those two formulations reveal quite specific discomfort with adoption. The idea of someone's giving up parental rights to a baby somehow seems "unnatural," even frightening. Did our parents ever want to give us up?

regret we had been born? Haven't we wanted at various times to turn our backs on our own children? Has parenting always seemed "worth it"? The idea of giving up parental rights is threatening not only to biological parents but also to adoptive. One reason Sarah and Mat Taine's giving up parental rights to their new son was so upsetting to us was that it realized an option we had had with Ruth but never even admitted to ourselves. Parent-child relationships are problematic—that's reality—but then so is all love of any duration. Fairy tales end with the very beginning of a union; otherwise they wouldn't be fairy tales.

And then there is the other side of adoption: the idea of parenting a child who's not related by blood seems so unselfish, so risky, that it ceases to be normal parenting and becomes "doing good." After all, would our parents really love us if they weren't our parents? Would we love our children if they weren't our children? At times doesn't it seem that it's only the blood tie that holds us all together? The mistake here, it seems to me, lies in taking the phrase "blood tie" literally. It is, after all, an *idea* of connectedness. "Blood tie" is a metaphor—a metaphor for the emotional bond of family members, a bond that is generally accepted as capable of withstanding a great deal of tension. The fact that some adopted people go through their whole lives not knowing they are adopted suggests how easily a person's concept of his or her biological background can be replaced by the image of another. It's the image of the bond that's important, rather than a literal reality. In one sense, perhaps, nonadoptive parents don't give themselves sufficient credit. When a nonadoptive mother with guilt says to herself, "This child is obnoxious; I don't really *like* him. I would never love him if he weren't my son," she's not appreciating the fact that her feeling he's her child is her emotional construction, that that very fact shows, among other things, her love. This is one way, perhaps, in which adoptive parents have it easier. They don't make that mistake.

Our society defines the family with the phrase "blood tie." The only metaphors that are powerful enough to carry the weight of our feelings as parents are biological ones. Thus it is quite understandable how Ken and I describe our experience of losing Jonathan, our experience with Nicholas and Ruth. The loss of Jonathan was a "stillbirth." Nicholas and Ruth are "of our blood." For a couple of years after Nicholas and Ruth were born I had recurring dreams about their births. They were fragmentary dreams—I'd wake up feeling as though there was a mystery I couldn't solve, that perhaps I wasn't remembering something fully or correctly. When the children were just three, I had what seems to have been the last, at least so far, of my birth dreams. I dreamed that after considerable struggle, I finally discovered why it was I couldn't remember—however much I tried—the actual experience of my children's birth. I had wanted natural childbirth, I'd been promised that I wouldn't be given any drugs, but I had finally discovered that, in fact, both times I'd been drugged, totally put out. They hadn't told me before because they were afraid I'd be angry that they hadn't followed my directions. It wasn't anger but incredible relief that I felt; the mystery of my lack of memory was finally solved. Dreams, fictions, metaphors, are ways we as human beings can express emotional realities.

Nicholas and Ruth are children of our own. Ken is their real father. I am their real mother. There is nothing about my identity that I know in a more primal way. Then what does it matter if much of society speaks of the "real mother" as the birth mother, "children of one's own" as biological children? To a great extent it doesn't. What is most essential to parenting takes place in a private realm; it is at most glimpsed, deduced, assumed, by people outside a family. But there is, also, a public realm—where we act in a public way as our child's mother or father. That's part of the parent package—not the substance of it, but nonetheless not something easily dismissed. When someone presumes, acts as though, I'm not Nicholas's or Ruth's real mother, that public role is denied me. It's normal, I think, that I would resent that.

I have the fear, also, that my children will internalize some of society's attitude. But, I remind myself, the friends I have who were adopted children and much of the recent research indicate that that happens with surprising infrequency. The responses to one question in Leslie Stein's interviews suggest that the nonadopted adolescents she talked to thought of adoption as problematic in a way that adopted adolescents did not. The other day, I was asked by an acquaintance, somewhat out of the blue, if Nicholas and Ruth had ever asked about their real mothers. I was watching the children and not quite focusing on our conversation. And it took me several moments to figure out what she was asking. The emotional reality I knew simply blocked out other presumptions. And if that's my reality and Ken's—and is reinforced, as it is, by friends and family—I know it almost certainly will also be our children's reality.

In the end, when I think about our story, I have only one regret about adopting our children—and with it comes a poignant sense of limitation. It is not that I never bore a child physically. It is something else, something

I didn't fully appreciate *until* I adopted. The regret is that—the emotional reality of my dream aside—I couldn't bear *these* two children, Nicholas and Ruth. Even if, somehow, I bore a biological child, he or she *wouldn't* be Nicholas or Ruth.

Adoptive parents know that though it seems to their baby that they are the whole world, they are not. He or she will gradually learn that they are limited, that they are not all-powerful. Every parent, of course, knows that. It is just, I feel, that adoptive parents know their limitation with a particular poignance. I think of Nicholas and Ruth, at almost four, who are fascinated by how long and hard we, their parents, worked to get them, how frightened we were that something would go wrong and we would lose them, how overwhelming it was for us finally to be able to hold our babies in our arms. They know they are a source of joy—and they love that. But they have no understanding that there is any other possible mother in the universe for them than me, any other father than Ken. Conceptually, as well as emotionally, we *are* their beginning. They will at some point, however, understand that their physical beginning was elsewhere. They will understand that their parents can't give them everything, that in fact they *have* not given them everything. We did not give them the breath of life.

But that does not diminish us as parents. After all, a parent's understanding that it is impossible to be everything to a child is a necessary component of the best that he or she can give to a child—a love that nurtures the child's sense of himself as a separate being, a love that is great enough to refuse to possess. That is the love that creates not the breath of life but the abundance of life.

And, finally, in order to have these particular two children, Nicholas and Ruth, I would—any day—give up the ability to have physically conceived them. That seems a small price to pay. There is one little girl in their pre-school who has curly, fair hair like mine. Not so long ago, a mother whom I didn't know said to me as we were both racing in to pick up our children on time, "I know who's mother you are. She looks exactly like you." The little girl in question is a very nice child, but, still, I felt a rush of gratitude for my fate as I thought of my two extraor-dinarily beautiful, uniquely different, and uniquely mine, straight-dark-haired children.

A few months ago I read an adopted child's description of how awkward he found the school assignment to draw a family tree. He dutifully drew a diagram of his adoptive family's tree but felt it wasn't really his. If adoption in-volves "genetic amputation"—as stated by one book on adoption, ostensibly sympathetic to it, that I recently picked up in a bookstore—then his discomfort is clearly to be expected. And this is the image that unfortunately, I feel, our society endorses. But there is another metaphor for adoption that seems to me to be much more accurate. The adopted child is a scion grafted onto another tree. He brings with himself the genetic makeup of his original tree and unites it with a new stock—both becoming a part of that new one and changing it. What grows is something to be prized. To quote a character in Shakespeare's *The Winter's Tale,* of which I am particularly fond, "This is an art / Which does mend nature—change it rather—but / The art itself is nature." I feel it is a mistake, it is unnatu-ral, to deny the genetic otherness an adopted child pos-sesses, but it is tragic, and fully as unnatural, not to see how that otherness grows a part of something new. Nicho-las and Ruth are not simply our children; they are our parents' grandchildren. They connect us to the past, our parents, and they connect us to the future. They are buds grafted by love onto another tree, a tree that grows new and fertile through them.

❧ Afterword: 1989

The questions we were asked while we were adopting our children made me feel that ideally one should have answers to all the questions, know how to be a parent before becoming one. But changing and growing with one's children, it seems to me, is an inevitable part of parenting. I am not exactly the same as I was several years ago when I finished writing this book.

I wrote the book when the pain of those long years of infertility was still raw and our children almost too miraculous to be real. Recently I reread what I had written and was surprised at how long ago that time seemed. The book chronicles the story of our becoming parents. Right now we are busy being just that. We are immersed in the logistical problems, the emotional ups and downs, of being a two-career family with two demanding, bewitching, adored, children. I am amazed by the energy needed to make even the small decisions with which we are constantly faced. Should Nicholas be forced to go to Ruth's piano recital? (We decided no.) Should Ruth be allowed to play soccer when Nicholas feels it's *his* game? (We decided yes.) What limits should be placed on Nicholas's desire to tie up the whole inside of the house in a spider web of twine and rope? Should we protect Ruth from the fact that her hamster died in the washing machine? Like most parents, we complain: chauffeuring, homework, wet mittens marking the dining room table, Nicholas's fetish for junk mail, Ruth's reluctance to eat with anything but her fingers. A few days ago I was so tired of the clutter in our house that I dumped into trash bags everything lying around on tables, counters, and chairs, put the bags in the basement, and waited to see if either child would miss anything. But even as I stomped to the basement, I thought of how it would feel not to have the wet mittens or the clutter, not to have our children. My exasperation was mixed with gratitude—a lasting gift of infertility.

I still have some feelings, of course, about my inability to get pregnant. When people talk about pregnancy, I feel a bit awkward, a little left out. But I'm no longer aware of a sense of loss. In the last chapter I spoke of my dream of giving Nicholas and Ruth birth. It supplied a powerful, comprehensible form to the emotions that had reshaped my life. That dream no longer carries such significance. Adoption—from this side of it—was like going to sleep one night and waking up with an expanded consciousness, an expanded identity. Who would have thought I was capable of having a Chinese son and a Colombian daughter! There is something exhilarating about introducing a whole new genetic pool into one's family tree—which is what adoption is—that I would not want to give up. At times I am jealous of people with three children, but I am not of women who are pregnant. A few years ago I would not have believed how nonessential for me pregnancy would eventually seem.

I also would not have believed that I would enjoy talking to my children about their birth parents. In spite of how I thought I should feel, I dreaded the beginning of their questions. The first specific one came several years ago at dinner from Ruth: "Mama, did I grow in your tummy?" When I answered, "You know you grew in another woman's tummy," she responded in a characteristic, earthy four-year-old way: "Yuck, it must have smelled." That ended the discussion for the moment. It had not occurred to me that the subject could be funny. The children now, of course, have a much fuller understanding of and interest in their birth parents. Ken and I find we don't simply wait for them to ask questions. Talking about their birth is intimate — it rarely occurs when outsiders are around — and binding, a shared imagining of a past profoundly important to each of us. Far from making me feel inadequate, it makes me feel close to my children, a primary participant in their emotional, imaginative worlds. I can't imagine feeling more significant, more essential, if I had physically borne them.

Looking back on the years of infertility and trying to adopt, I am aware of things I would now do differently. I regret that we did not try harder to learn about our children's birth parents. We may not have been able to gather much more information, but our fears that the adoptions would fall through made our efforts perfunctory. In each case we were able to think of little beyond the present extraordinary baby. I did not understand that information which then seemed a frightening reminder of the partialness of our claim to our babies would not carry such connotations just a few years later. Our circumstances led us to be more concerned about our claim to our children than we should have been, but perhaps many parents begin with a sense of possession. We have learned that parenting doesn't mean creating a child's identity, but nurturing it. Parenting doesn't mean possession. Everything about our children's identities is now important to us. And I am sorry they — and we — can't know all the particulars of their biological roots.

One reviewer of the book remonstrated that adoption need not be as difficult as it was for us. That is true. When we began looking into adoption, support and information were less readily available than today. But also, for a long time, as the reviewer gently suggested, we weren't open to what was there. We aren't unusual in that. As important as support groups and information sources are, for many people there is much that is necessarily isolating and private about infertility and the decision to adopt. And in some ways the experience has not become easier. The medical developments of the last years are wonderful, but in the midst of all the breakthroughs — the *in vitro* procedure, new drugs, surrogate arrangements — it is easy to forget the reason for getting pregnant. With more and more scientific advancements it becomes more and more tempting to continue forever in infertility's vicious cycle of hope and despair. It may be even harder emotionally for the infertile person now than it was a few years ago.

There is, moreover, no question in my mind that many people in our society are uncomfortable with the idea of adoption. The other day Ruth came into the kitchen dragging a friend who was over for the day. "Becky doesn't believe I live with my real parents," she said with amusement. "Will you tell her I do?" Becky stood there embarrassed, simply not understanding this strange phenomenon, adoption. Recently a friend, an adoptee, told me of her astonishment at discovering her husband of twelve years still didn't quite believe she could feel her adoptive family was her real family. A few years ago that would have upset me. Now I too can laugh. I know the reality from inside the experience.

Rereading the book brings back the memory of the emptiness of those years without children. Our years now are rich with life. I think of last summer and Nicholas's excitement at catching his first fish, which so surprised him that he flung his pole at the silvery, dashing shape. Or of Ruth in the early morning, leaning over me, a book from my own childhood in her hand, watching impatiently for my eyes to open—her signal to jump into bed and insist I continue reading to her. I think of last Mother's Day, when I put our children to bed and thanked them for making it such a nice day. Nicholas responded in a typical burst of enthusiasm: "I'm going to make *every day* of your life Mother's Day." He has—they have.